Divine Love Made Flesh

Divine Love Made Flesh

~

The Holy Eucharist as the Sacrament of Charity

RAYMOND LEO CARDINAL BURKE

Catholic Action for Faith and Family
SAN DIEGO

Cover photograph: Monstrance used at the
Shrine of Our Lady of Guadalupe,
founded by Raymond Leo Cardinal Burke
La Crosse, Wisconsin (www.guadalupeshrine.org)
Designed and Crafted by Granda (www.granda.com)

Photograph of Cardinal Burke,
by Jim Breen (www.midentity.tv)

Cover design: Devin Schadt
Typesetting: Loyola Book Composition
Printed in the United States of America
ISBN 978-0-9816314-2-4

Acknowledgments

Thomas McKenna and Anthony DeBellis of Catholic Action for Faith and Family

Reverend Michael J. Houser

Sister M. Regina van den Berg, F.S.G.M.

~

Catholic Action for Faith and Family is a lay organization inspired by the teachings of the Roman Catholic Church and dedicated to upholding and promoting the ideals of Christian Civilization.

Contents

Introduction

Blessed Pope John Paul II described the mission of the Church in our day with the words, "the new evangelization." He recognized that the Church in our time is called and sent to carry out her mission in a very challenging societal and cultural context. In his teaching during the more than twenty-six years of his service as the Vicar of Christ on earth, Blessed Pope John Paul II insistently urged us all, according to our vocation in life and our particular personal gifts, to take up the work of the new evangelization. In his Post-synodal Apostolic Exhortation *Christifideles laici*, "On the Vocation and the Mission of the Lay Faithful in the Church and in the World," he described what he called the "hard test" which living the Catholic faith is today in a practically atheistic world, in a culture marked by secularism:

> Whole countries and nations where religion and the Christian life were formerly flourishing and capable of fostering a viable and working community of faith, are now put to a hard test, and in some cases, are even undergoing a radical transformation, as a result of a constant spreading of an indifference to religion, of secularism and atheism. This particularly concerns countries and nations of the so-called First World, in which economic well-being and consumerism, even if coexistent with a tragic situation of poverty and misery, inspires and sustains a life lived "as if God did not exist." This indifference to religion and the practice of religion devoid of true meaning in the face of life's very serious problems, are not less worrying and upsetting when compared with declared atheism.[1]

---

[1] Blessed Pope John Paul II, Post-synodal Apostolic Exhortation *Christi-*

It is through participation in the Holy Eucharist that we best understand what we must do to carry out the new evangelization, namely pour out our lives in union with Christ. At the same time, we are nourished with the incomparable spiritual food of the Body, Blood, Soul and Divinity of Christ, which strengthens us to carry out His mission in the world. In the words of a decree of the Second Vatican Ecumenical Council, drawing upon a text of Saint Thomas Aquinas, in the Holy Eucharist "is contained the whole spiritual good of the Church, namely Christ himself our Pasch and the living bread which gives life to men through his flesh—that flesh which is given life and gives life through the Holy Spirit."[2] In the celebration of the Holy Eucharist, in the words of the same Decree, "men are invited and led to offer themselves, their works and all creation with Christ."[3]

Because the Holy Eucharist is the source of our life in the Church and its highest expression, I thought it good to write a commentary on Blessed John Paul II's final Encyclical Letter *Ecclesia de Eucharistia*, "On the Eucharist in its Relationship to the Church," published on Holy Thursday, April 17, 2003, and on our Holy Father Pope Benedict XVI's Postsynodal Apostolic Exhortation *Sacramentum Caritatis*, "On the Eucharist as the Source and Summit of the Church's Life and Mission," published on February 22, 2007, the Feast of the Chair of Saint Peter. *Sacramentum Caritatis* is the fruit of the Eleventh Ordinary Assembly of the Synod of Bishops, which was celebrated October 2–23, 2005.

---

fideles laici, "On the Vocation and the Mission of the Lay Faithful in the Church and in the World," December 30, 1988, n. 34a.

[2] Vatican Council II, Decree *Presbyterorum Ordinis*, "On the Ministry and Life of Priests," n. 3. English translation: Austin Flannery, O.P., ed., *Vatican Council II: The Conciliar and Post Conciliar Documents*, Collegeville, Minn.: Liturgical Press, 1975, p. 871.

[3] *Ibid.*

It is my hope that, as you read this book, you will obtain a copy of both the Encyclical Letter *Ecclesia de Eucharistia* and the Apostolic Exhortation *Sacramentum Caritatis*. It is also my hope that the teaching contained in the two documents, presented in this commentary, will lead you to a more profound appreciation of our life in Christ in His Mystical Body, the Church, especially through the Holy Eucharist, and be for you a source of new enthusiasm and new energy for carrying out the new evangelization.

Context of the Synod of Bishops on the Eucharist

The Eleventh Ordinary Assembly of the Synod of Bishops was convoked by Pope Benedict XVI's predecessor, Blessed Pope John Paul II, as part of his extraordinary effort, at the end of his pontificate, to promote the knowledge and love of the Most Blessed Sacrament. In *Ecclesia de Eucharistia*, a complete and remarkably striking presentation of the Church's teaching on the Holy Eucharist, Blessed Pope John Paul II announced a forthcoming "more specific document" on the care to be taken in observing the norms of the Sacred Liturgy.[4]

By mandate of Blessed Pope John Paul II, the Instruction *Redemptionis Sacramentum*, "On Certain Matters to Be Observed or to Be Avoided Regarding the Most Holy Eucharist," was prepared by the Congregation for Divine Worship and the Discipline of the Sacraments with the help of the Congregation for the Doctrine of the Faith, at the head of which the future Pope Benedict XVI was then serving.

---

[4] Blessed Pope John Paul II, Encyclical Letter *Ecclesia de Eucharistia*, "On the Eucharist in its Relationship to the Church" [hereafter *Ecclesia de Eucharistia*], April 17, 2003, n. 52.

Blessed Pope John Paul II approved the Instruction and "ordered it to be published and to be observed immediately by all concerned"[5] on March 19, 2004.

Year of the Eucharist

Blessed Pope John Paul II then announced the Year of the Eucharist to be observed from October 2004 to October 2005. The inspiration for the Year of the Eucharist, he explained, "came from two events" which served "to mark its beginning and end,"[6] that is, the International Eucharistic Congress which took place October 10–17, 2004, in Guadalajara, Mexico, and the Ordinary Assembly of the Synod of Bishops which was held in the Vatican October 2–23, 2005, on the subject of the Holy Eucharist. Blessed Pope John Paul II also asked that World Youth Day, celebrated in Cologne, Germany, August 16–21, 2005, be centered on the Holy Eucharist. Regarding World Youth Day 2005, he wrote: "I would like the young people to gather around the Eucharist as the vital source which nourishes their faith and enthusiasm."[7]

The context of the Synod of Bishops was nothing less than the Holy Spirit at work through the Shepherd of the Universal Church to help us all to grow in our knowledge and love of the greatest gift which is ours in the Church,

---

[5] Congregation for Divine Worship and the Discipline of the Sacraments, Instruction *Redemptionis Sacramentum*, "On Certain Matters to Be Observed or to Be Avoided Regarding the Most Holy Eucharist," March 19, 2004, n. 186.

[6] Blessed Pope John Paul II, Apostolic Letter *Mane Nobiscum Domine*, "For the Year of the Eucharist," October 7, 2004, n. 4.

[7] *Ibid.*

Blessed Pope John Paul II approved the Instruction and "ordered it to be published and to be observed immediately by all concerned"[5] on March 19, 2004.

Year of the Eucharist

Blessed Pope John Paul II then announced the Year of the Eucharist to be observed from October 2004 to October 2005. The inspiration for the Year of the Eucharist, he explained, "came from two events" which served "to mark its beginning and end,"[6] that is, the International Eucharistic Congress which took place October 10–17, 2004, in Guadalajara, Mexico, and the Ordinary Assembly of the Synod of Bishops which was held in the Vatican October 2–23, 2005, on the subject of the Holy Eucharist. Blessed Pope John Paul II also asked that World Youth Day, celebrated in Cologne, Germany, August 16–21, 2005, be centered on the Holy Eucharist. Regarding World Youth Day 2005, he wrote: "I would like the young people to gather around the Eucharist as the vital source which nourishes their faith and enthusiasm."[7]

The context of the Synod of Bishops was nothing less than the Holy Spirit at work through the Shepherd of the Universal Church to help us all to grow in our knowledge and love of the greatest gift which is ours in the Church,

---

[5] Congregation for Divine Worship and the Discipline of the Sacraments, Instruction *Redemptionis Sacramentum*, "On Certain Matters to Be Observed or to Be Avoided Regarding the Most Holy Eucharist," March 19, 2004, n. 186.

[6] Blessed Pope John Paul II, Apostolic Letter *Mane Nobiscum Domine*, "For the Year of the Eucharist," October 7, 2004, n. 4.

[7] *Ibid*.

It is my hope that, as you read this book, you will obtain a copy of both the Encyclical Letter *Ecclesia de Eucharistia* and the Apostolic Exhortation *Sacramentum Caritatis*. It is also my hope that the teaching contained in the two documents, presented in this commentary, will lead you to a more profound appreciation of our life in Christ in His Mystical Body, the Church, especially through the Holy Eucharist, and be for you a source of new enthusiasm and new energy for carrying out the new evangelization.

Context of the Synod of Bishops on the Eucharist

The Eleventh Ordinary Assembly of the Synod of Bishops was convoked by Pope Benedict XVI's predecessor, Blessed Pope John Paul II, as part of his extraordinary effort, at the end of his pontificate, to promote the knowledge and love of the Most Blessed Sacrament. In *Ecclesia de Eucharistia*, a complete and remarkably striking presentation of the Church's teaching on the Holy Eucharist, Blessed Pope John Paul II announced a forthcoming "more specific document" on the care to be taken in observing the norms of the Sacred Liturgy.[4]

By mandate of Blessed Pope John Paul II, the Instruction *Redemptionis Sacramentum*, "On Certain Matters to Be Observed or to Be Avoided Regarding the Most Holy Eucharist," was prepared by the Congregation for Divine Worship and the Discipline of the Sacraments with the help of the Congregation for the Doctrine of the Faith, at the head of which the future Pope Benedict XVI was then serving.

---

[4] Blessed Pope John Paul II, Encyclical Letter *Ecclesia de Eucharistia*, "On the Eucharist in its Relationship to the Church" [hereafter *Ecclesia de Eucharistia*], April 17, 2003, n. 52.

I

ECCLESIA DE EUCHARISTIA

The Eucharist, Mystery of Faith

In the Introduction of the Encyclical Letter *Ecclesia de Eucharistia*, Blessed Pope John Paul II expressed the desire to "rekindle" our wonder at the Eucharist, "the source and summit of the Christian life."[1]

Rekindling our wonder at the Holy Eucharist is at the heart of the new evangelization to which we are called at the dawn of a new Christian millennium. Blessed Pope John Paul II made clear to us, in his Apostolic Letter *Novo Millennio Ineunte*, that the program of the new evangelization is Christ Himself.[2] The Holy Father instructs us to contemplate the face of Christ, to recognize His presence with us in the Church, most of all in the Sacrament of His true Body and Blood, and so to become more and more like Christ in our daily living.

Eucharistic Sacrifice

After the consecration of the bread and wine, that is after the bread and wine have become truly and completely the Body and Blood of Christ, and after the priest has shown

---

[1] *Ecclesia de Eucharistia*, n. 6.
[2] Cf. Blessed Pope John Paul II, Apostolic Letter *Novo Millennio Ineunte*, "At the Close of the Great Jubilee of the Year 2000," January 6, 2001, n. 29.

the Body and Blood of Christ to the congregation and has
adored Christ by genuflecting before the Sacred Host and
the Precious Blood, he immediately invites the congregation
to proclaim the mystery of faith. The congregation then
sings or says, "We proclaim Your Death, O Lord, and profess Your Resurrection, until You come again" or one of the
other memorial acclamations which all have the same content: Christ's Passion and Death, His Resurrection and His
Return in Glory at the end of time. The memorial acclamation reflects the deepest truth about the Holy Eucharist: its
inseparability from the Passion, Death, and Resurrection of
Christ.

Christ instituted the Holy Eucharist on the night He was
betrayed, the night before His cruel Passion and Death. He
did so in order that the fruits of His Suffering and Dying on
the Cross, on the next day, would be constantly offered in
the Church, to all peoples of every time and place. The Mass
is, as Blessed Pope John Paul II reminded us, "not only a re-
minder but the sacramental re-presentation"[3] of our Lord's
Passion and Death. Christ desired that the sacrifice which
He was going to offer at Calvary on Good Friday continue
always in the Church, and He fulfills His desire by the most
wondrous sacrament of the Holy Eucharist, in which He,
acting through His minister, the ordained priest, offers ever
anew the one sacrifice of His life on the Cross. Blessed Pope
John Paul II stated in a striking manner the inseparability
of the Sacrifice of the Mass and the Sacrifice of Calvary:

> This sacrifice [of Calvary] is so decisive for the salvation of
> the human race that Jesus Christ offered it and returned to
> the Father only *after he had left us a means of sharing in it* as

---

[3] *Ecclesia de Eucharistia*, n. 11.

if we had been present there. Each member of the faithful can thus take part in it and inexhaustibly gain its fruits.[4]

The Holy Eucharist is indeed the "inestimable gift" of Christ to us, before which the only fitting response is adoration. The celebration of the Holy Mass truly makes us present at the sacrifice of Calvary.

The Holy Eucharist is not just one of the many gifts which Christ has left to us in the Church. It is the gift of Christ's true Body and Blood, the gift of the whole fruit of His saving Passion and Death.[5] All the other gifts of Christ to us are only fully understood in relationship to the gift of the Eucharistic Sacrifice and Banquet. That is why Blessed Pope John Paul II rightly first turns to the teaching on the Holy Eucharist in assisting us to carry out the new evangelization.

Christ's Universal Charity

Contemplating the face of Christ at the Lord's Supper and at every celebration of the Mass, we contemplate His love, the incarnation of Divine Mercy which "knows no measure."[6] When Christ instituted the Holy Eucharist, He declared the bread to be His Body *given for us* and the wine to be His Blood *poured out for us*. The Holy Eucharist is not simply a partaking in the Body and Blood of Christ, not simply a banquet, but is always, at the same time, a sharing in Christ's sacrifice. The Heavenly Bread, which is the Holy Eucharist, is essentially sacrificial: it is the Body and Blood of Christ, offered and poured out for us as He gave up His life for us

---

[4] *Ibid.*
[5] Cf. *Ibid.*
[6] *Ibid.*

on the Cross. The sacrifice of the Cross is perpetuated at every celebration of the Mass. Communion with the Body and Blood of Christ is always participation in Christ's Suffering and Dying. It is important to understand that the sacrifice of Christ is one. "The Eucharist thus applies to men and women today the reconciliation won once for all by Christ for mankind in every age."[7] This is the great wonder and treasure of the Holy Mass. The Mass is not an additional sacrifice to Calvary. It is not a constant multiplication of the one sacrifice of Calvary. It *is* the sacrifice of Calvary, it is Calvary's "commemorative representation," which, by the universal charity of Christ, makes his "one, definitive redemptive sacrifice always present in time."[8]

In the Sacrifice of Calvary, Christ offered Himself completely to God the Father. God the Father, in response to the total obedience of His Son, gave Christ eternal life by raising Him from the dead. In the Eucharistic Sacrifice, Christ makes present in an unbloody manner the Sacrifice of Calvary. We, the Church, sharing in Christ's sacrifice, are called to offer ourselves in union with Christ. We are called to share in His universal charity, which knows no measure. Through the Holy Eucharist, God the Father responds to our sacrifice with the gift of eternal life.

The Real Presence

Blessed Pope John Paul II reminds us: "The Eucharistic Sacrifice makes present not only the mystery of the Saviour's passion and death, but also the mystery of the resurrection

---

[7] *Ecclesia de Eucharistia*, n. 12.
[8] *Ibid.*

- 2 -

The Eucharist Builds the Church

Introduction

After having reflected upon the Holy Eucharist as the mystery of faith (Chapter One), Blessed Pope John Paul next considers the Holy Eucharist as the source of the strength and growth of the Church.

Blessed Pope John Paul II was inspired by the teaching of the Second Vatican Ecumenical Council, which reminds us that the work of our Redemption continues to be carried out in the Church, principally by the offering of the Sacrifice of the Mass. The teaching of the Council also underlines for us the truth that the unity of all the faithful in the one Body of Christ is "both expressed and brought about"[1] in the celebration of the Holy Eucharist. The importance of the Holy Eucharist for the life of the Church, from her very beginnings, cannot be emphasized enough.

At the Beginnings of the Church

The celebration of the Holy Eucharist was, in fact, the source of the life of the Church at her very beginnings. On the night

---

[1] Vatican Council II, Dogmatic Constitution *Lumen Gentium*, "On the Church," n. 3, in *Ecclesia de Eucharistia*, n. 21.

before He died, Christ, in the company of the Apostles, instituted the Holy Eucharist, in order that, through the priestly ministry of the Apostles, the faithful might always share in the spiritual fruits of the sacrifice which He would carry out on Calvary on the following day, Good Friday. The twelve Apostles, symbolically recalling the twelve tribes of Israel, represent the new People of God, embracing all the nations, called to life from the pierced Heart of Christ and sustained in life from the glorious Heart of Christ, now seated at the right hand of the Father. The Last Supper, which is the First Eucharist, "laid the foundations of the new messianic community, the People of God of the New Covenant,"[2] just as the sacrifice at Mount Sinai had sealed the Old Covenant. We can rightly say that Christ constituted the Church at her beginnings at the Last Supper.

When our Lord transformed the bread and wine of the Last Supper into His true Body and Blood, He made possible our communion with Him through the Most Blessed Sacrament. Through the institution of the Holy Eucharist, our Lord made it possible for us to become one body with Him. Our Lord instructed the Apostles to renew His Supper, so that the People of God might be built up in every time and place through communion with Him, that is, communion in His true Body and Blood.[3]

Our Holy Father makes clear the profound meaning of Eucharistic communion for our life in the Church by reminding us that not only do we receive Christ in Holy Communion, but He also receives us. Christ truly calls us friends by inviting us to the Eucharistic Sacrifice and Banquet. In other words, Christ deeply desires that we be in His com-

---

[2] Cf. *Ecclesia de Eucharistia*, n. 21.
[3] Cf. *Ecclesia de Eucharistia*, n. 21.

pany and that He be in our company, and He fulfills His desire, best of all, through the Eucharistic Banquet and Sacrifice.

Communion with Christ in the Holy Eucharist has enabled the Church, from her very beginnings, to carry out her mission of being a sign of salvation in Christ for all the nations. The Church is constituted to carry out the mission of Christ in the world. Christ alive within the Church continues His saving work. The Holy Father recalls the definitive words of our Lord Jesus: "As the Father has sent me, even so I send you" (*Jn* 20:21). At the celebration of the Holy Mass, the Church receives her mission which is to share in the mystery of Christ's Suffering, Dying and Rising from the Dead. At the same time, at the Mass, she also expresses most fully the same mission of bringing all mankind into communion with God—Father, Son and Holy Spirit.

Confirming the Church in Unity

Participation in the Eucharistic Sacrifice and Banquet sustains the Church in the unity which her members enjoy because of Baptism. All of the Church's members are incorporated into Christ, they become truly members of the Body of Christ, through the waters of Baptism. The Holy Eucharist nourishes the life of Christ within us from the moment of our baptism. It is in virtue of our unity with Christ in Baptism and in the Eucharist that we are also one with each other. The Holy Eucharist confirms the unity of the many members of Christ.[4]

The unity of the Church has its source in the "joint and

---

[4] Cf. *Ecclesia de Eucharistia*, n. 23.

inseparable activity of the Son and of the Holy Spirit."[5] The Church is called into being through Christ's Passion, Death and Resurrection, by which He has won the outpouring of the Holy Spirit upon us, her members.

Christ was conceived by the Holy Spirit in the womb of the Blessed Virgin Mary. Christ became incarnate for our salvation through the action of the Holy Spirit. It is also the Holy Spirit who overshadows our gifts of bread and wine at the Mass, transforming them into the true Body and Blood of Christ. The Holy Spirit unceasingly nourishes and strengthens His life within us through the incomparable spiritual food which is the Body and Blood of Christ.

The Holy Eucharist binds brothers and sisters in Christ in the deepest possible unity, far beyond any merely human bond. Participation in the Eucharistic Sacrifice and Banquet is not merely sharing a meal together. Rather, it is sharing in the divine communion which alone can bring mankind to unity and peace.[6]

There is in us, at one and the same time, the deepest desire of communion with one another and the tendency to division, what Blessed Pope John Paul calls the "seeds of disunity,"[7] due to original sin and our actual sins. The Holy Eucharist fulfills our desire for unity with one another in a way beyond all our imagining; it makes us one with each other in the divine Son of God. Our unity with one another has its origin in God. It cannot be destroyed by any human force and has its eternal fulfillment in the life which is to come.

At the same time, the Holy Eucharist strengthens us, so

---

[5] *Ecclesia de Eucharistia*, n. 23.
[6] Cf. *Ecclesia de Eucharistia*, n. 24.
[7] *Ecclesia de Eucharistia*, n. 24.

that we may purify ourselves of the seeds of disunity. Communion with Christ strengthens us to overcome, with Christ, the division which sin always introduces into our lives. Here we see the essential connection of the Holy Eucharist and Penance. Through the confession of our sins, which separate us, in varying degrees, from God and from one another, we are prepared to receive the Body and Blood of Christ, uniting us to God and to each other. At the same time, receiving the Body and Blood of Christ enlightens our minds and inflames our hearts to see what keeps us from unity with God and with each other, and to root out from our hearts these seeds of disunity.

Worship of the Eucharist
Outside of the Mass

In the context of reflecting upon how the celebration of the Holy Eucharist builds up the life of the Church, Blessed Pope John Paul II underlined the importance of worship of the Blessed Sacrament outside of Mass. He reminded us that the Real Presence of Christ under the species of bread and wine, from the moment of the Consecration of the Mass, remains as long as the species themselves remain, and that, therefore, the Church reserves the Body of Christ in the tabernacle after the distribution of Holy Communion.

The reserved Blessed Sacrament comes directly from the Sacrifice of the Mass and inspires the desire for Holy Communion, also for spiritual communion when it is not possible to receive sacramental communion. So important is worship of the Blessed Sacrament that Blessed Pope John Paul reminded bishops and priests of their responsibility "to encourage, also by their personal witness, the practice of Eucharistic adoration, and exposition of the Blessed Sacrament in particular, as well as prayer of adoration before Christ under the Eucharistic species."[8]

Blessed Pope John Paul draws our attention to the profound reality of prayer before the Blessed Sacrament. It is spending time with the Lord. He likens it to the experience of the Beloved Disciple who rested his head on the breast of the Master. Through prayer before the Blessed Sacrament, we experience the inexhaustible love of the glorious Sacred Heart of Jesus, from which Christ unceasingly pours forth His grace upon us.

In *Novo Millennio Ineunte*, the Apostolic Letter at the conclusion of the Great Jubilee of the Year 2000, Blessed Pope John Paul II reminded us that our time requires, above all, that we be persons of prayer. In other words, he taught us that the new evangelization will be accomplished, first of all, through the power of prayer. As we know the need of more intense prayer in our lives, we sense the need to pray in the presence of our Eucharistic Lord. The Holy Father exclaims: "How often, dear brothers and sisters, have I experienced this, and drawn from it strength, consolation and support!"[9]

Church teaching urges us to pray before the Blessed Sacrament. The example of the saints inspires us to treasure, in a most special way, Eucharistic adoration. Blessed Pope John Paul II quotes Saint Alphonsus Liguori: "Of all devotions, that of adoring Jesus in the Blessed Sacrament is the greatest after the sacraments, the one dearest to God and the one most helpful to us."[10]

---

[8] *Ecclesia de Eucharistia*, n. 25.

[9] *Ibid.*

[10] Saint Alphonsus Liguori, *Visite al SS. Sacramento e a Maria Santissima*, Introduction: *Opere Ascetiche* (Avellino, 2000), p. 295, in *Ecclesia de Eucharistia*, n. 25.

the Holy Eucharist. Blessed Pope John Paul II did not live to celebrate either World Youth Day 2005 or to preside at the Synod of Bishops on the Eucharist. His successor, Pope Benedict XVI, who had worked so closely with Blessed Pope John Paul II during most of his pontificate, carried forward his extraordinary work on the Holy Eucharist.

In reading *Ecclesia de Eucharistia* and *Sacramentum Caritatis*, we should keep in mind the great love for the Church, for us, the living members of the Church, which inspired Blessed Pope John Paul II to convoke and Pope Benedict XVI to conduct the Synod of Bishops for the purpose of promoting Eucharistic faith and practice. At the conclusion of *Ecclesia de Eucharistia*, Blessed Pope John Paul II wrote these words to us:

> In the humble signs of bread and wine, changed into his body and blood, Christ walks beside us as our strength and our food for the journey, and he enables us to become, for everyone, witnesses of hope. If, in the presence of this mystery, reason experiences its limits, the heart, enlightened by the grace of the Holy Spirit, clearly sees the response that is demanded, and bows low in adoration and unbounded love.[8]

May these words of the most beloved and great Blessed Pope John Paul II inspire our reading of *Ecclesia de Eucharistia* and *Sacramentum Caritatis* and our practice of the Faith in all the different places, ways, and vocations in which the members of the Body of Christ live and carry out the mission of the Church.

---

[8] *Ecclesia de Eucharistia*, n. 62.

Conclusion

Through the Holy Eucharist, first of all by participation in the Sacrifice of the Mass and then by Eucharistic worship outside of Mass, we contemplate the Face of Christ as directly and fully as is possible for us on this earth. From our contemplation of the Face of Christ, we will draw the grace to live in Christ every day. It is the Holy Eucharist, above all, which builds up the Church in unity and love.

- 3 -

The Eucharist Is Apostolic

Introduction

In the beginning of the third chapter of *Ecclesia de Eucharistia*, Blessed Pope John Paul II reminded us that the relationship between the Church and the Holy Eucharist is so intimate that the marks of the Church—one, holy, catholic and apostolic—also describe the Holy Eucharist. He then devotes the third chapter to a reflection upon the apostolic character of the Holy Eucharist.[1]

Apostolic in Three Senses

Blessed Pope John Paul II described the three meanings which the apostolic character or apostolicity of the Church has. First of all, it means that the Church "was and remains built"[2] upon the foundation of the Apostles. So, too, the Holy Eucharist was entrusted by Christ to the Apostles and has come to us through the unbroken succession of the apostolic ministry.

Secondly, apostolicity means that the Church hands on the deposit of faith, received from the Apostles. So, too, the Church celebrates the Holy Eucharist "in conformity with

---

[1] Cf. *Ecclesia de Eucharistia*, n. 26.
[2] *Ecclesia de Eucharistia*, n. 27.

the faith of the Apostles."[3] The Holy Father points out that
the teaching authority of the Church has necessarily defined
"more precisely" the doctrine on the Holy Eucharist, in order to remain true to the faith of the Apostles. He states:
"This faith remains unchanged and it is essential for the
Church that it remain unchanged."[4]

Thirdly, the Church is apostolic because the Bishops, successors to the Apostles, teach, sanctify and guide the Church.
They carry out the apostolic ministry in communion with the
Holy Father, Successor of Saint Peter, Head of the Apostles,
and with the assistance of priests who share in their apostolic ministry. The existence of the Church depends upon
the unbroken succession of the apostolic ministry. The Holy
Eucharist also depends upon the apostolic ministry of the
Apostles and their successors, for it is only the ordained
priest, acting in the person of Christ, who can offer the Eucharistic Sacrifice on behalf of all the faithful. The third
sense of the apostolic nature of the Holy Eucharist helps us
to understand the reason why only the priest recites the Eucharistic Prayer, "while the people participate in faith and
in silence."[5]

In the Person of Christ

The ordained priest offers the Eucharistic Sacrifice in virtue
of the Sacrament of Holy Orders, by which he is configured
to Christ, Shepherd and Head of God's flock. The ordained
priest does not take the place of Christ in the offering of the
Holy Eucharist, but Christ acts in him. In other words, the
Holy Eucharist remains always the action of Christ. The

---

[3] *Ibid.*
[4] *Ibid.*
[5] *Ecclesia de Eucharistia*, n. 28.

Holy Eucharist can be offered "in the person of Christ"[6] only in virtue of the sacramental grace of Holy Orders. For that reason, the manner of the priest, in offering the Mass, should always point to the person of Christ and not to the person of the priest.

The congregation gathered for the celebration of the Holy Eucharist requires the ministry of the priest. The priestly ministry is necessary, so that the celebration of the Mass is one with the sacrifice of Calvary and the Last Supper or First Eucharist, for Christ acts in the priest. The congregation by itself, that is without the presence of the priest, is incapable of renewing the Eucharistic Sacrifice.[7]

The most important responsibility of a bishop, therefore, is to ordain priests, so that they may offer the Eucharistic Sacrifice for God's holy people. The ordination of a priest by a successor of the Apostles means that the ordained priest is a gift received from Christ Himself.[8]

Ecumenical Reflections

The reflection upon the relationship of the ordained ministry to the Eucharistic Sacrifice points to a significant area of division between the Roman Catholic Church and the Ecclesial Communities which have sprung up in Europe and beyond, beginning with the Protestant Revolt in the sixteenth century. The Second Vatican Ecumenical Council reminded us that, because these Ecclesial Communities do not have the Sacrament of Holy Orders, they have not preserved the Sacrifice of the Mass in its integrity.[9]

---

[6] *Ecclesia de Eucharistia*, n. 29.
[7] Cf. *Ibid.*
[8] Cf. *Ibid.*
[9] Cf. *Ecclesia de Eucharistia*, n. 30.

It is because of the significant difference of belief regarding the Holy Eucharist that Catholics are not permitted to receive the communion which is given in these Ecclesial Communities. Otherwise, a serious question could be raised about the Catholic faith in the Holy Eucharist, causing confusion about a central doctrine of the faith. For the same reason, it is never permissible to substitute participation in an ecumenical prayer service or in the liturgical services of one of the non-Catholic Ecclesial Communities for participation in Sunday Mass. While participation in ecumenical services can help prepare us for a fuller unity, it cannot replace Eucharistic communion.[10]

Finally, the Holy Father points out that the restriction of the power to consecrate the Holy Eucharist to Bishops and priests alone "does not represent any belittlement of the rest of the People of God, for in the communion of the one body of Christ which is the Church this gift redounds to the benefit of all."[11]

Center of the Priestly Ministry

The Holy Eucharist is the heart and the highest expression of the Church. It is, therefore, also "the center and summit of priestly ministry."[12] The Holy Eucharist, in fact, is the reason for the existence of the priestly ministry which Christ instituted at the Last Supper.

The Holy Father sensitively observes that the volume and variety of priestly activities and the fast pace of life in society, in general, could easily cause a loss of focus on the part

---

[10] Cf. *Ibid.*

[11] *Ibid.*

[12] *Ecclesia de Eucharistia*, n. 31.

of priests. The pastoral charity, which is expressed in every truly pastoral act of a priest, comes chiefly from the Holy Eucharist. For that reason, the priest necessarily seeks in the Eucharistic Sacrifice and in Eucharistic worship outside of Mass the direction and strength for all of his pastoral activity. The heart of the priestly ministry in the Eucharistic Sacrifice explains also the Church's desire that a priest offer Mass daily, even if he is without a visible congregation, for the Mass is always "an act of Christ and the Church."[13] As one of my professors of Canon Law observed, a priest never offers the Mass alone, for the whole company of Heaven assists at every offering of the Mass.

The priest who centers his whole priestly life and ministry on the Holy Eucharist will overcome the tendency to lose his focus because of the many demands of his pastoral office. He will not become overwhelmed by the demands of his priestly ministry, for he will be united with Christ in bringing Christ's pastoral charity to God's flock.

Given all of the above, it is clear that the Holy Eucharist must be at the center of the formation of future priests. First of all, the manner in which a priest celebrates the Mass and brings the Holy Eucharist to others outside of Mass will inspire very much those whom God is calling to the ordained priesthood. The manner of participation of all of the faithful will also contribute very much in assisting a young man to recognize the call to the priesthood and to respond to it wholeheartedly. Those called to the priesthood will discover God's call before the Blessed Sacrament, through frequent and attentive participation in Holy Mass and through daily Eucharistic devotion.

In the context of the place of the Holy Eucharist in the life

---

[13] Decree *Presbyterorum Ordinis*, n. 14, in *Ecclesia de Eucharistia*, n. 31.

of the Catholic community and the necessity of the Eucharistic ministry of the ordained priest, the Holy Father reflects upon the great distress caused to the Church by situations in which a congregation of the faithful is without a priest. It will be very difficult for those called to the priesthood to recognize God's call without the active involvement of the priest, especially his offering of the Mass.[14]

The Holy Father refers to the various temporary solutions to the situation of a congregation without a priest. Prepared members of the laity or prepared consecrated persons, drawing upon the common grace of Baptism, lead the faithful in a prayer on Sunday and may distribute Holy Communion consecrated at an earlier celebration. What is essential is to point out always to the congregation that the situation is temporary and that the congregation must pray and sacrifice, so that God calls more young men to the ordained priesthood. The serious deficiency of the situation should inspire everyone to develop and use all of the resources needed for an effective apostolate of priestly vocations.[15]

Finally, the Holy Father points out that the laity or consecrated persons who share in the pastoral care of the parish are obliged to do all that they can to foster the love of the Holy Eucharist among the faithful and their desire to participate in the Mass, celebrated by a validly ordained priest. In this way, as the Holy Father observes, the congregation will never miss the opportunity to participate in the Holy Mass offered by Christ through the ministry of His priest.

---

[14] Cf. *Ecclesia de Eucharistia*, n. 32.
[15] *Ibid.*

Conclusion

Our continuing reflection upon the Holy Eucharist leads us to preserve the integrity of our Eucharistic faith in our relationships with members of non-Catholic Ecclesial Communities, so that we do not compromise, in any way, our witness to the Holy Eucharist, God's most wonderful gift to us in the Church. Likewise, it leads us to an ever deeper love of the vocation to the ordained priesthood and to the pastoral service of priests, above all in the offering of the Eucharistic Sacrifice.

- 4 -

The Eucharist Is Communion

Introduction

The Second Vatican Ecumenical Council emphasized very much the nature of the Church as communion. The Council presents, with a particular richness, the teaching regarding the Church, what is technically called ecclesiology, and views the Church, most of all, as the instrument for safeguarding and fostering our communion with God—Father, Son and Holy Spirit—and our communion with one another as members of the Church.

In the celebration of the Holy Eucharist the Church expresses best her identity as communion and most fully carries out her mission of safeguarding and fostering communion. Therefore, it should not surprise us that one of the most common names given to the Holy Eucharist is Communion. Blessed Pope John Paul II devotes the fourth chapter of his Encyclical to the discussion of the relationship of the Holy Eucharist to communion with God and communion among the faithful in the Church.[1]

Desire of the Holy Eucharist

There can be no fuller communion with God than the Holy Eucharist, in which we receive the Body of Christ, God the

---

[1] Cf. *Ecclesia de Eucharistia*, n. 34.

Son made man for our salvation. For the person of faith, all other goods in life are seen always in relationship to the Holy Eucharist, the greatest good in our life. The measure of the depth of our faith is naturally the strength of our desire to receive Holy Communion.

Blessed Pope John Paul II reminds us that the practice of making a spiritual communion flows from the deep desire of receiving the Body of Christ. Spiritual communion is the expression of our conscious desire to receive the Body of Christ. Actually, an act of spiritual communion prepares us fittingly for the time when we are able to receive sacramental communion. Whenever we experience a period of time during which we are unable to receive Holy Communion, and sense the strong need of the Holy Eucharist to sustain us, we express in prayer our desire. God responds to our act of spiritual communion with the help of His grace. Regarding spiritual communion, Blessed Pope John Paul II quotes Saint Teresa of Jesus:

> When you do not receive communion and you do not attend Mass, you can make a spiritual communion, which is a most beneficial practice; by it the love of God will be greatly impressed on you.[2]

The Church's tradition includes a number of beautiful prayers for making a spiritual communion. One such prayer is that of Saint Alphonsus Liguori:

> My Jesus, I believe that Thou art present in the Blessed Sacrament. I love Thee above all things and I desire Thee in my soul. Since I cannot now receive Thee sacramentally, come at least spiritually into my heart. As though

---

[2] Saint Teresa of Jesus, *Camino de Perfección*, Chapter 35, in *Ecclesia de Eucharistia*, n. 34.

Thou wert already there, I embrace Thee and unite myself wholly to Thee; permit not that I should ever be separated from Thee.[3]

Invisible Dimension of Communion

The Holy Father rightly points out that the Holy Eucharist sustains and develops a certain communion which must necessarily precede it and which it expresses. The communion which participation in the Holy Eucharist presupposes has both invisible and visible dimensions.

The invisible dimension is the life of grace within us. It is only by God's grace that we have communion with Him and with one another. God, for His part, gives us the virtues of faith, hope and love, and, we, for our part, cultivate these virtues and the moral virtues by which we, with the help and under the guidance of the Holy Spirit, become more like Christ.

The invisible dimension of communion which is the presupposition of Eucharistic communion demands that we examine ourselves before approaching the Holy Eucharist and that, if we are conscious of having committed a grave sin, we seek reconciliation with God in the Sacrament of Penance before receiving Holy Communion.[4]

The Sacraments of the Holy Eucharist and Penance are intimately related to one another. Communion in the Body of Christ necessarily inspires daily conversion of life, which is greatly helped through frequent confession. With the ardent desire of the Holy Eucharist comes also a deep sorrow

---

[3] Saint Alphonsus Maria de' Liguori, "An Act of Spiritual Communion," in *The Raccolta* (New York: Benziger Brothers, 1957), p. 96.

[4] Cf. *Ecclesia de Eucharistia*, n. 36.

over the ways in which we offend God and one another. The response to sorrow for sin, even our venial sins, is reconciliation with God and with the Church, which is God's gift to us in the Sacrament of Penance. Grave or mortal sin prohibits our reception of Holy Communion, until we have received God's forgiveness of our sin in the Sacrament of Penance. However, Eucharistic communion will more and more inspire within us the desire to confess also our venial sins, lest we grow complacent or lukewarm in our love of the Eucharist.

Each of us must examine his or her conscience regarding the state of grace, which is required to receive Holy Communion. The Holy Father also mentions the case of public conduct which is "seriously, clearly and steadfastly contrary to the moral norm,"[5] and before which the Church is obliged to deny Holy Communion. Such action of the Church is required in order to respect properly the Holy Eucharist and to avoid confusion and scandal in the community of faith.

Visible Dimension of Communion

The visible dimension of the communion which is the precondition for Eucharistic communion is the bonds of the doctrine of the faith, the sacraments and Church governance.[6] Reception of the Body of Christ is the manifestation of fullness of communion in the Church and, therefore, demands visible bonds of communion with the Church. Therefore, it is never permitted to give Holy Communion to someone who dissents from the truth of faith regarding the Holy Eucharist or who is unbaptized.[7]

---

[5] *Ecclesia de Eucharistia*, n. 37.
[6] Cf. *Ecclesia de Eucharistia*, n. 35.
[7] Cf. *Ecclesia de Eucharistia*, n. 38.

which crowned his sacrifice."[9] Christ can only become the Bread of Life for us because He is risen from the dead and is alive for us in the Church. We refer to the living presence of Christ with us in the Holy Eucharist as the Real Presence. In order to help us understand more fully the meaning of the Real Presence, our Blessed Pope John Paul II returned to a text of Pope Paul VI who explained that the term does not imply that the other presences of Christ in the Church are "not real," but underlines that the Eucharistic Presence "is a presence in the fullest sense: a substantial presence whereby Christ, the God-Man, is wholly and entirely present."[10]

The proper term for the change of the bread and wine into the Body and Blood of Christ, which takes place during the Holy Mass, is *transubstantiation*. No other term has been found to be as adequate in pointing to the Eucharistic mystery. Theologians and saints, down through the Christian centuries, have desired to plumb ever more the depth of the mystery of the Eucharist, of the profound reality which *transubstantiation* expresses. Often, too, their love of the Holy Eucharist and desire to express their love has taken poetic form, for example, the hymn of Saint Thomas Aquinas: *Adoro Te devote* ("Devoutly I adore You"), to which our Blessed Pope John Paul II referred. Once again, Pope Paul VI underlines the truth which must be reflected in all thinking, speaking and writing about the Holy Eucharist:

> Every theological explanation which seeks some understanding of this mystery, in order to be in accord with Catholic faith, must firmly maintain that in objective reality, independently of our mind, the bread and wine have ceased to exist after the consecration, so that the adorable

---

[9] *Ecclesia de Eucharistia*, n. 14.
[10] *Ecclesia de Eucharistia*, n. 15.

body and blood of the Lord Jesus from that moment on are really before us under the sacramental species of bread and wine.[11]

Eucharistic Banquet

Christ makes Himself substantially present to us through the Holy Eucharist principally so that we may receive Him in Holy Communion. "The Eucharistic Sacrifice is intrinsically directed to the inward union of the faithful with Christ through communion."[12] The Holy Eucharist is true spiritual food, Christ nourishing the life of the Holy Spirit within us through the reception of His glorious Body and Blood. The sixth chapter of the Gospel of Saint John helps us very much to understand the Eucharistic Banquet. Christ made it clear that only by eating His Body and drinking His Blood do we have life within us. The disciples understood the true importance of His teaching, for, from that day, some refused to believe and left His company.

Holy Communion, participation in the Eucharistic Banquet, is Christ's way of sustaining His life poured out within us at the moment of our baptism, and strengthened and increased within us from the moment of our confirmation. The Sacraments of Initiation—Baptism, Confirmation and the Holy Eucharist—are essentially related to one another. "Thus by the gift of his body and blood Christ increases within us the gift of his Spirit, already poured out in Baptism and bestowed as a 'seal' in the sacrament of Confirmation."[13]

---

[11] Pope Paul VI, *Solemn Profession of Faith*, June 30, 1968, 25: *Acta Apostolicae Sedis* 60 (1968), 442–44, in *Ecclesia de Eucharistia*, n. 15.

[12] *Ecclesia de Eucharistia*, n. 16.

[13] *Ecclesia de Eucharistia*, n. 17.

Conclusion

Communion in the Body and Blood of Christ is already now a participation in the fullness of communion with God, which will be ours in the Heavenly Kingdom. The Holy Eucharist is likewise the Spiritual Food to sustain us along life's pilgrimage home to God the Father. In the wonderful words of Saint Ignatius of Antioch, Holy Communion is "a medicine of immortality, an antidote to death."[14] That is why the Church so much desires that the dying receive Holy Communion and calls the Holy Communion of the dying by a special name, *Viaticum*, food for the journey from this life to the next.

The fact that Holy Communion is an anticipation of the life to come also means that it commits us to preparing the day of Christ's Final Coming during each moment of our lives. The account of the institution of the Holy Eucharist in the Gospel of Saint John underlines the mandate which the Holy Eucharist is for us. It is a sharing in the outpouring of Christ's life out of love for us and for all; it contains the command to wash the feet of our brothers and sisters. Blessed Pope John Paul II concludes the first chapter of *Ecclesia de Eucharistia* with these inspiring words:

> Proclaiming the death of the Lord "until he comes" (*1 Cor* 11:26) entails that all who take part in the Eucharist be committed to changing their lives and making them in a certain way completely "Eucharistic."[15]

---

[14] Saint Ignatius of Antioch, *Ad Ephesios*, 20: *Patrologia Graeca* 5, 661, in *Ecclesia de Eucharistia*, n. 18.

[15] *Ecclesia de Eucharistia*, n. 20.

tion of the Holy Eucharist be faithfully observed. He reminded us that the Sacred Liturgy is never the private possession of the priest or the community, and speaks of the deep suffering caused to the faithful by abuses introduced into the celebration of the Mass. Our observance of liturgical law is a fundamental expression of love of Christ and of the Church.

Conclusion

Because of the importance of the fitting and dignified celebration of the Holy Mass, Blessed Pope John Paul II, with the help of the Roman Curia, prepared a special document on the matter, namely, the Instruction *Redemptionis Sacramentum*, "On Certain Matters to Be Observed or to Be Avoided Regarding the Most Holy Eucharist." He concluded Chapter Five of *Ecclesia de Eucharistia* with words which should inspire our own great care in approaching the Eucharistic Sacrifice and Banquet: "No one is permitted to undervalue the mystery entrusted to our hands: it is too great for anyone to feel free to treat it lightly and with disregard for its sacredness and its universality."[11] We cannot redesign the Holy Eucharist or exploit it for our own purposes. The Holy Eucharist is always, at one and the same time, Sacrifice, Banquet and Real Presence.

---

[11] *Ibid.*

- 6 -

At the School of Mary

Introduction

In the final chapter of his Encyclical Letter *Ecclesia de Eucharistia*, Blessed Pope John Paul II reminded us that, if we want to ponder the profound mystery of the Holy Eucharist, especially its relationship with the Church, then we must look to Mary, Mother of the Church and also model of the Church. Blessed Pope John Paul II, in his Apostolic Letter *Rosarium Virginis Mariae*, "On the Holy Rosary," had already reminded us that our Blessed Mother is our first and best teacher in contemplating the Face of Christ. Recall that the fifth of the Luminous Mysteries of the Rosary is the Institution of the Eucharist, for Mary helps us best to look upon the Face of Christ by leading us to the Holy Eucharist. Blessed Pope John Paul II observed: "Mary can guide us towards this most holy sacrament, because she herself has a profound relationship with it."[1] Even as Mary always leads us to Christ, her Son, so she will lead us to the Blessed Sacrament, the true Body and Blood of her Son.

Mary guides us to the Holy Eucharist in two ways. First of all, our Blessed Mother certainly participated in the Holy Mass from the very beginning of the Church's life, even as she was present with the Apostles in the Cenacle after the

---

[1] *Ecclesia de Eucharistia*, 53.

Resurrection, praying with them for the Descent of the Holy Spirit. By exercising her ecclesial maternity, Mary leads us to the Holy Eucharist.

Mary also guides us to Christ in the Blessed Sacrament by the whole manner of her life, which can aptly be described as Eucharistic. Mary is, above all, a *"woman of the Eucharist."* In this way, she is the model of the Church. By her Eucharistic manner of life, Mary invites us "to imitate her in her relationship with this most holy mystery."[2]

Disposition of Faith

The Holy Eucharist is a mystery of faith, which goes beyond our capacity to understand and requires that we trust completely in the Word of Christ. Mary teaches us to grow in the theological virtue of faith. Her disposition of faith, which we are called to imitate, is perhaps best expressed in the Gospels in her words to the wine stewards at the Wedding Feast of Cana: "Do whatever he tells you" (*Jn* 2:5). Mary shows her maternal care of us by urging us to go to Christ, to put our faith in Him, to trust in His words spoken at the Last Supper, that is, to believe that the Eucharistic species of the bread and wine are, in truth, the Body and Blood of Christ.[3]

We see Mary's disposition of faith in her response to the Archangel Gabriel at the Annunciation. At her words, "Let it be done to me as you say," God the Son came into the world by becoming incarnate in her womb through the overshadowing of the Holy Spirit. At the moment of the Incarnation, Mary anticipated what happens for us faithful at

---

[2] *Ibid.*

[3] Cf. *Ecclesia de Eucharistia*, n. 54.

every Eucharist: Christ becomes present for us, under the species of bread and wine, so that we may receive Him into our very being. Blessed Pope John Paul II points out the profound similarity between Mary's belief in the words of the Archangel Gabriel and our belief in approaching Holy Communion. When the priest announces, "The Body of Christ," we respond "Amen." Our "Amen" is like Mary's "*Fiat* (Let it be done)."[4]

Mary expressed already the Church's faith in the Holy Eucharist at the moment of the Incarnation. She became, as Blessed Pope John Paul II states, "the first 'tabernacle' in history—in which the Son of God, still invisible to our human gaze, allowed himself to be adored by Elizabeth, radiating his light as it were through the eyes and the voice of Mary."[5] Reflecting upon the relationship between Mary's faith at the Annunciation and Birth of our Lord, and our own faith in the Holy Eucharist, we are inspired to express ever deeper devotion and love every time we are blessed to be in the presence of the Blessed Sacrament or to receive Holy Communion.

Sacrifice

Mary also anticipated, by her whole life, the Church's share in the sacrifice of Christ through the Holy Eucharist. Just as we are most perfectly united with Christ through participation in the Holy Eucharist, so Mary, from the very moment of the Incarnation, poured out, with her Incarnate Son, her entire life. Simeon had expressed the sacrificial nature of Mary's divine maternity when she presented our Lord in

---

[4] *Ecclesia de Eucharistia*, 55.
[5] *Ibid.*

the Temple. Simeon stated so directly: "A sword of sorrow will pierce your own heart" (*Lk* 2:34–35). Her participation in Christ's Suffering and Death reached its fullness at the foot of the Cross.

Her share in Christ's sacrifice, after His Death and Resurrection, was continued through her participation in the Holy Mass. Blessed Pope John Paul II exclaims: "The body given up for us and made present under sacramental signs was the same body which she had conceived in her womb!"[6] Who, then, can better teach us to unite ourselves to the sacrifice of Christ in the Holy Eucharist than Mary? She leads us to unite our hearts, like her Immaculate Heart, to the Sacred Heart of Jesus, poured out in perfect love of God and of neighbor.

Memorial

Blessed Pope John Paul II reminded us that all that Christ accomplished for us on Calvary is made present for us in the Holy Mass. This is the meaning of His words: "Do this in remembrance of me" (*Lk* 22:9). Therefore, at every Eucharist, Christ once again gives Mary to us as our Mother and gives us to her as her true sons and daughters, as He did when He died on the Cross for us.[7]

Concretely, this means a commitment on our part to be faithful students at the School of Mary, to permit Mary to exercise fully her maternal care of us, so that we may become more and more like Christ. Our Blessed Mother is always with us at every celebration of the Holy Eucharist. The Church never celebrates the Holy Eucharist without commemorating our Blessed Mother, present with us, lead-

---

[6] *Ecclesia de Eucharistia*, n. 56.
[7] Cf. *Ecclesia de Eucharistia*, n. 57.

ing us to Christ, and instructing us to be obedient to what He tells us.[8]

Eucharistic Attitude

Blessed Pope John Paul II invited us to pray the *Magnificat*, Mary's prayer at the Visitation, while meditating upon the great gift of the Holy Eucharist. In the *Magnificat*, we find expressed in a most wonderful way Mary's Eucharistic attitude and way of being.

The *Magnificat* is a prayer of praise and thanksgiving, as is every celebration of the Holy Eucharist for us. With Mary, we praise God through Jesus, our Savior, but also we praise God in Jesus and with Jesus. We praise God for all His wonders, but most of all for that greatest of His wonders, the Incarnation.

Finally, the *Magnificat* expresses the hope for and anticipation of "the new heavens" and "the new earth,"[9] at Christ's Final Coming. At every celebration of the Holy Eucharist, we experience already the grace which will be fully ours on the Last Day. We experience the truth about our lives and our world, namely that we are made for final glory, we are made to share fully in Christ's glory, the glory He won for us on Calvary. The Holy Eucharist is the pledge of our future destiny in and with Christ.

Conclusion

Blessed Pope John Paul II concluded the Encyclical Letter with an expression of gratitude to God for the twenty-five

---

[8] Cf. *Ibid.*
[9] *Ecclesia de Eucharistia*, n. 58.

years of his exercise of the ministry of Saint Peter in the
Church. He offered his own testimony of faith in the Most
Blessed Sacrament. He told us of how the Holy Eucharist
has been at the heart of His priestly life and ministry.

Before the Holy Eucharist, our senses fail us. Our senses
fail to identify the truth of the Holy Eucharist. Faith, however, is sufficient for us to know the truth and profess the
truth of the Eucharist.[10]

In the Holy Eucharist, we come to understand the truth
about our own earthly journey, our pilgrimage home to God
the Father. The truth is that our pilgrimage is with and in
Christ. In Him, we live the life of the Holy Trinity and we
transform the world, according to God's plan. Blessed Pope
John Paul II recalled his insistence, in his Apostolic Letter *Novo Millennio Ineunte*, that the answer to the meaning
of our life pilgrimage is not some new program but rather
the person of Christ. The perfection of our life is found in
knowing, loving and imitating Christ. Where do we most
find Christ and come to understand the mystery of His life
for us? It is the Holy Eucharist. Blessed Pope John Paul II
wrote: "In the Eucharist, we have Jesus, we have his redemptive sacrifice, we have his resurrection, we have the
gift of the Holy Spirit, we have adoration, obedience and
love of the Father."[11]

The Holy Eucharist also expresses most perfectly the ecumenical dimension of our faith, our response with Christ,
"that all may be one" (*Jn* 17:11). The Holy Eucharist increases our desire for full unity with all our brothers and
sisters with whom we share Baptism. But it also places before our eyes the real demands of communion in faith and

---

[10] Cf. *Ecclesia de Eucharistia*, n. 59.
[11] *Ecclesia de Eucharistia*, n. 60.

apostolic succession, the many hurdles which must be overcome before we are fully one with our Christian brothers
and sisters.

Blessed Pope John Paul II reminded us that we can never
show too much care and reverence for the Holy Eucharist,
for in it is contained the grace of our salvation. He invited
us once again to contemplate the Face of Christ in the Holy
Eucharist through the eyes of Mary, His Mother and our
Mother. At the School of Mary, we will never lose any of
our wonder before the great mystery of faith, which is the
Holy Eucharist.

I close with words of Blessed Pope John Paul II:

> In the humble signs of bread and wine, changed into his
> body and blood, Christ walks beside us as our strength and
> our food for the journey, and he enables us to become, for
> everyone, witnesses of hope. If, in the presence of this mys-
> tery, reason experiences its limits, the heart, enlightened by
> the grace of the Holy Spirit, clearly sees the response that
> is demanded, and bows low in adoration and unbounded
> love.[12]

May our minds and hearts never fail in wonder and love
before the Holy Eucharist, Christ with us now, Christ the
pledge of our future glory.

---

[12] *Ecclesia de Eucharistia*, n. 62.

II

SACRAMENTUM CARITATIS

- 7 -

The Sacrament of Charity

Pope Benedict XVI opens the Post-synodal Apostolic Exhortation *Sacramentum Caritatis* by reminding us that the Holy Eucharist is the sacrament of charity because it is "the gift that Jesus Christ makes of himself, thus revealing to us God's infinite love for every man and woman."[1] Our Lord poured out His life for us on the Cross at Calvary, the supreme sacrifice which He makes ever new for us in the Sacrament of the Holy Eucharist. Our Holy Father recalls how our Lord washed the Apostles' feet at the Last Supper to signify His humble and unfailing love of them. Having washed the Apostles' feet, He instituted the Holy Eucharist, so that He might love them and us—and, indeed, all men and women of every time and place—totally and "to the end" (*Jn* 15:13). Referring to the Last Supper, Pope Benedict XVI exclaims:

> What amazement must the Apostles have felt in witnessing what the Lord did and said during that Supper! What wonder must the eucharistic mystery also awaken in our own hearts![2]

---

[1] Pope Benedict XVI, Post-synodal Apostolic Exhortation *Sacramentum Caritatis*, "On the Eucharist as the Source and Summit of the Church's Life and Mission" [Hereafter: *Sacramentum Caritatis*], February 22, 2007, n. 1.
[2] *Ibid.*

The Holy Father's words remind us that the action of the Holy Mass is one with the Last Supper and the Lord's Sacrifice on Calvary.

By the Holy Eucharist, our Lord remains with us always. In the words of Pope Benedict XVI, "the Lord meets us, men and women created in God's image and likeness (cf. *Gen* 1:27), and becomes our companion along the way."[3] Our Eucharistic Lord is the food of truth and freedom for our earthly pilgrimage, the spiritual nourishment which we most need and desire for our happiness in this life and our eternal happiness in the life to come.

In the Holy Eucharist, we best and most fully know the love of God for us. The Holy Eucharist unveils the truth about God's love for us and nourishes, within us, the freedom to love as God loves. If we have lost a sense of wonder and profound gratitude before the Eucharistic Sacrifice and the Real Presence of our Lord Jesus Christ in the consecrated Host, then we do not recognize the truth which is before our eyes. In the ancient cultures, "eternal wisdom" was seen as the "real food" which man seeks and which "truly nourishes him as man."[4] In Christ, through the Eucharistic Sacrifice, man receives eternal wisdom in person. Christ gives His Body, Blood, Soul and Divinity to us through the Eucharistic Sacrifice. In the Holy Eucharist, we have communion with the wisdom of God incarnate.

Pope Benedict XVI reminds us that our sharing in the Eucharistic Sacrifice is precisely a sharing in Christ's own self-offering. In the symbolic language of the Bible, God espouses man through the Holy Eucharist. Man shares in

---

[3] *Sacramentum Caritatis*, n. 2.

[4] Pope Benedict XVI, Encyclical Letter *Deus Caritas Est*, "On Christian Love," December 25, 2005, n. 13.

the very love of God, having communion with God through the Body and Blood of Christ, and, therefore, communion with Him in the outpouring of His life in love of us.

The Holy Father refers to the "sacramental mysticism"[5] of the Holy Eucharist. Through the Eucharistic Sacrifice, we have mystical communion with God, which is founded on the reality of the Real Presence. The communion is profoundly mystical and profoundly real.

Development of the Eucharistic Rites

Our Lord comes to us in the Holy Eucharist through the Rite of the Mass and other Eucharistic rites. The rites of the Church, and above all the Rite of the Mass, point to the reality of our Lord's abiding presence with us. Pope Benedict XVI notes the "richness and variety"[6] of the liturgical rites, both historically in the Latin Church and in the Churches of the East, by which our Lord makes always new His Eucharistic Sacrifice. He reminds us that all of the approved rites, inspired by the Holy Spirit, manifest a unity; that is, they are the historical development of the one action of the Mass.

Commenting on the liturgical renewal which "began with the Second Vatican Ecumenical Council,"[7] our Holy Father expressed the gratitude of the Bishops for the fruits of the renewal. Acknowledging the many benefits of the liturgical renewal, He also acknowledged the "difficulties and even occasional abuses"[8] in the actual carrying out of the renewal.

---

[5] *Ibid.*
[6] *Sacramentum Caritatis*, n. 3.
[7] *Ibid.*
[8] *Ibid.*

In that regard, he affirmed the conviction of the Bishops at the Synod that the "riches" of the renewal "are yet to be fully explored."[9]

The Holy Father then addressed a central point regarding the historical development of the liturgical rites in the Latin Church. The changes in the liturgical rites, introduced after the Council, could be seen as something entirely new, that is, as having no relationship to the liturgical rites which the changes were adopted to renew. Such a perception is completely false. The changes can only be understood in the context of the organic development of the rites of the Sacred Liturgy, along the Christian centuries, true to the promptings of the Holy Spirit. Pope Benedict XVI states:

> Concretely, the changes which the Council called for need to be understood within the overall unity of this historical development of the rite itself, without the introduction of artificial discontinuities.[10]

A change in the Sacred Liturgy which is not a development of the rites of the Church as they have come down to us could not be the work of the Holy Spirit.

A concrete example of an organic development in the Sacred Liturgy is the rich development of Eucharistic adoration in the Middle Ages. After the Second Vatican Ecumenical Council, some believed that the development of Eucharistic adoration was to be set aside as somehow not essentially related to the action of the Mass. Regarding the question, Pope Benedict XVI refers to an address which he gave to the members of the Roman Curia on December 22, 2005. In the address, he spoke about the whole richness

---

[9] *Ibid.*
[10] *Ibid.*

of the teaching and activity of Blessed Pope John Paul II, regarding the Most Blessed Sacrament, and also about the Synod of Bishops on the Holy Eucharist, which had just concluded a month earlier. In particular, he mentioned the false opposition seen by some in our time between the Eucharistic Sacrifice and Eucharistic adoration. He concludes:

> Receiving the Eucharist means adoring the One Whom we receive. Precisely in this way and only in this way do we become one with Him. Therefore, the development of Eucharistic adoration, as it took shape during the Middle Ages, was the most consistent consequence of the Eucharistic mystery itself: only in adoration can profound and true acceptance develop. And it is precisely this personal act of encounter with the Lord that develops the social mission which is contained in the Eucharist and desires to break down barriers, not only the barriers between the Lord and us but also and above all those that separate us from one another.[11]

The Holy Father shows how the significant development of Eucharistic adoration in the Middle Ages was not in discontinuity with the Sacred Liturgy but, rather, was an organic development in the rites by which the Eucharistic mystery has been and is celebrated in the Church.

What is the Synod of Bishops?

Pope Benedict XVI next comments on the work of the Eleventh Ordinary Assembly of the Synod of Bishops in the context of the apostolic ministry of his predecessor, Blessed

---

[11] Pope Benedict XVI, Christmas Message to the Roman Curia, "Christmas, the Council and conversion in Christ," *L'Osservatore Romano, Weekly Edition in English*, January 4, 2006, p. 5.

Pope John Paul II. In the introduction to this book, I com-
mented briefly on the context of the work of the Synod. The
Holy Father also describes the context of the intense effort
of Blessed Pope John Paul II to foster Eucharistic faith and
devotion. He reminds us that the Synod of Bishops, devoted
to the Holy Eucharist, concluded with the solemn Mass at
which Pope Benedict XVI canonized five saints "particularly
distinguished for their eucharistic piety: Bishop Józef Bil-
czewski, Fathers Gaetano Catanoso, Zygmunt Gorazdowski
and Alberto Hurtado Cruchaga, and the Capuchin Fra Fe-
lice da Nicosia."[12]

In order to understand the importance of *Sacramentum
Caritatis*, it will be helpful to reflect on the nature and purpose of the Synod of Bishops. From her beginnings, the
Church has employed the synod or council, a meeting called
by the Holy Father or Bishop or group of Bishops for the
purpose of seeking counsel on how best to provide for the
teaching of the faith, also in regard to particular situations in
the world, and for the fostering of ecclesiastical discipline.
The synod has its foundation in the sevenfold gift of the
Holy Spirit, which includes counsel.

At a synod, the members draw upon the gift of counsel,
offering practical suggestions to assist the Roman Pontiff,
Bishop or Bishops in the pastoral care and direction of the
flock. Not surprisingly, from the earliest times, the synod in
the Church has taken place in the context of solemn, public
prayer, calling upon the help of the Holy Spirit. Also, when
a synod is in preparation and in progress, all of the faithful
are asked to pray for the members, so that they speak only
what the Holy Spirit inspires in them.

Since the purpose of the synod is to offer counsel, the

---

[12] *Sacramentum Caritatis*, n. 4.

synod is not, in itself, a decision-making body. Rather, the synod offers to the Pope, Bishop, or Bishops recommendations which he or they use in giving pastoral care and direction.

The Synod of Bishops was instituted by Pope Paul VI, on September 15, 1965, during the final year of the Second Vatican Ecumenical Council, so that the fruits of the meeting of Bishops from throughout the world with the Roman Pontiff, experienced at the Council, could continue to be reaped. The Synod of Bishops is a solemn meeting of the Roman Pontiff with representative bishops from throughout the world to receive their consultation on questions of concern for the Church. The Synod of Bishops takes one of three forms: ordinary, extraordinary and special.

Ordinary Assembly of the Synod of Bishops

An "ordinary" assembly of the Synod of Bishops is convoked by the Holy Father "to foster closer unity between the Roman Pontiff and bishops, to assist the Roman Pontiff with their counsel in the preservation and growth of faith and morals and in the observance and strengthening of ecclesiastical discipline, and to consider questions pertaining to the activity of the Church in the world."[13] Blessed Pope John Paul II had convoked the Ordinary Assembly on the Holy Eucharist.

A meeting of the Synod of Bishops is "extraordinary" when it is called "to treat affairs which require a speedy solution."[14] For example, an extraordinary assembly of the Synod of Bishops was called by Blessed Pope John Paul II

---

[13] Can. 342.
[14] Can. 346, §2.

in 1985, on the occasion of the twentieth anniversary of the closing of the Second Vatican Council to address the reception of the teaching of the Council. One of the great fruits of that extraordinary assembly was the *Catechism of the Catholic Church*.

A meeting of the Synod of Bishops is "special," if it is made up of members of a particular portion of the Church. For example, a special assembly of the Synod of Bishops for America was held November 16 to December 12, 1997. Blessed Pope John Paul II promulgated the Post-synodal Apostolic Exhortation *Ecclesia in America*, the fruit of the Special Assembly, on January 22, 1999, in Mexico City. Similar special assemblies of the Synod of Bishops were convoked by Blessed Pope John Paul II for Africa, Asia, Europe and Oceania.

Fittingly, Blessed Pope John Paul II convoked an ordinary assembly, the Eleventh Ordinary Assembly, of the Synod of Bishops to assist him in promoting knowledge and love of the Most Blessed Sacrament. The text of the Post-synodal Apostolic Exhortation carries with it a special weight, for it is the fruit of a consultation of representative Bishops from every portion of the universal Church. It should also be noted that, according to the usual practice of the Roman Pontiff, prior to the actual celebration of the Synod, all Bishops were consulted and had the opportunity to submit their counsel in writing.

Conclusion

Pope Benedict XVI concludes the introductory chapter of *Sacramentum Caritatis* by describing the purpose of the document, namely, "to take up the richness and variety of the reflections and proposals which emerged from the recent

Ordinary General Assembly of the Synod of Bishops . . . and to offer some basic directions aimed at a renewed commitment to Eucharistic enthusiasm and fervor in the Church."[15] Basing himself on the desires expressed by the Bishops at the Synod, the Holy Father further specifies the purpose of the document as an encouragement of the faithful "to deepen their understanding of the relationship between the *Eucharistic mystery*, the *liturgical action*, and the *new spiritual worship* which derives from the Eucharist as the *sacrament of charity*."[16]

Finally, the Holy Father relates *Sacramentum Caritatis* to his Encyclical Letter *Deus Caritas Est*. Referring to the stress which he placed upon the Blessed Sacrament in *Deus Caritas Est*, Pope Benedict XVI reminds us that God expresses His love for us in bodily form, the Body and Blood of God the Son Incarnate, in the Holy Eucharist, so that He may spread His love "in us and through us."[17]

---

[15] *Sacramentum Caritatis*, n. 5.
[16] *Ibid.*
[17] *Deus Caritas Est*, n. 14.

- 8 -

The Holy Eucharist, Gift of the Holy Trinity

The Structure of *Sacramentum Caritatis*

Sacramentum Caritatis is divided into three parts: "The Eucharist, a Mystery to Be Believed," "The Eucharist, a Mystery to Be Celebrated," and "The Eucharist, a Mystery to Be Lived." The three parts address the Church's faith in the Holy Eucharist, her manner of celebrating the Eucharist, and her new life in Christ which has its source and highest expression in the Holy Eucharist.

Part One, "The Eucharist, a Mystery to Be Believed," begins by reminding us that the Holy Eucharist is the Mystery of Faith, for it contains the entire spiritual good of the Church, the Sacrifice and Real Presence of our Lord Jesus Christ. In the Holy Eucharist, we see the essential relationship between Catholic faith and the sacramental life. Our faith has its highest form of expression in the sacramental life. At the same time, our faith "is nourished and grows in the grace-filled encounter with the Risen Lord which takes place in the Sacraments."[1] Throughout the history of the Church, when there has been a strong Eucharistic faith and devotion, there has also been a deep commitment to live in

---

[1] *Sacramentum Caritatis*, n. 6.

Christ, to carry out the mission entrusted by Him into our hands.

Holy Eucharist, Gift of the Father

In the Holy Eucharist, we know the immeasurable love of God the Father for us. Pope Benedict XVI reminds us:

> In the Eucharist Jesus does not give us a "thing," but himself; he offers his own body and pours out his own blood. He thus gives us the totality of his life and reveals the ultimate origin of this love. He is the eternal Son, given to us by the Father.[2]

Our Holy Father recalls for us the words of our Lord Jesus in His Discourse on the Bread of Life in the Gospel according to Saint John. Our Lord declared:

> Truly, truly, I say to you, it was not Moses who gave you the bread from heaven; my Father gives you the true bread from heaven. For the bread of God is that which comes down from heaven, and gives life to the world (*Jn* 6:32–33).

As the discourse continues, our Lord Jesus identifies Himself with "the true bread from heaven" (*Jn* 6:32): "I am the living bread which came down from heaven; if any one eats of this bread, he will live forever; and the bread which I shall give for the life of the world is my flesh" (*Jn* 6:51). Reflecting upon the discourse, Pope Benedict XVI declares: "Jesus thus shows that He is the bread of life which the eternal Father gives to mankind."[3]

The Holy Eucharist is a share in the life of the Triune God. It is a gift which God—Father, Son and Holy Spirit

---

[2] *Sacramentum Caritatis*, n. 7.
[3] *Ibid.*

—alone can give. God the Father gives the gift through the Death and Resurrection of God the Son and the outpouring of the Holy Spirit. It is a gift given out of pure and selfless love, with total freedom. In the Holy Eucharist, God, the Holy Trinity, "who is essentially love (cf. *1 Jn* 4:7–8), becomes fully a part of our human condition."[4] Sharing in the life of the Holy Trinity, we, in our human condition, share in the communion of love of the three Persons in one God.

Holy Eucharist, the Lamb of God

God the Son Incarnate, our Lord Jesus Christ, fulfilled His vocation and completed His mission in the world by giving up His life for us on the Cross. In the crucified Body of Christ, "God's freedom and our human freedom met definitively in an inviolable, eternally valid pact."[5] Our Holy Father refers to a striking passage from his Encyclical Letter *Deus Caritas Est*, in which he expresses the mystery of God's love for us, revealed perfectly in the Passion and Death of Christ, and made always new for us in the Holy Eucharist: "Christ's death on the Cross is the culmination of that turning of God against Himself in which He gives Himself in order to raise man up and save him. This is love in its most radical form."[6]

Our Lord Jesus is the Paschal Lamb by Whom we are definitively saved from sin and nourished with the gift of God's love. At the very beginning of our Lord's public ministry, Saint John the Baptist identified Him as the "Lamb of God, who takes away the sin of the world" (*Jn* 1:29). Dying

---

[4] *Sacramentum Caritatis*, n. 8.
[5] *Sacramentum Caritatis*, n. 9.
[6] *Deus Caritas Est*, n. 12.

on the Cross, our Lord "freely gave himself in sacrifice for us, and thus brought about the new and eternal covenant."[7] What our Lord accomplished on the Cross, the fulfillment of God's promise of salvation, is ever new for us in the Holy Eucharist.

Our Lord instituted the Holy Eucharist at the Last Supper, on the night before His Passion and Death. Celebrating the Passover Meal, in which the People of God not only recalled their past deliverance from slavery but also prayed for "a yet more profound, radical, universal and definitive salvation,"[8] our Lord anticipated and made present the salvation from sin and everlasting death which He was to win for us by His death on the Cross and His Resurrection from the dead. The Crucifixion, Death and Resurrection of our Lord are, in fact, only fully understood in the context of the Lord's Supper, the Eucharistic Sacrifice and Banquet. Our Holy Father declares: "The institution of the Eucharist demonstrates how Jesus' death, for all its violence and absurdity, became in him a supreme act of love and mankind's definitive deliverance from evil."[9]

At the Last Supper, our Lord, the Lamb of God, commanded us: "Do this in remembrance of me" (*1 Cor* 11:24). In other words, our Lord "asks us to respond to his gift and to make it sacramentally present."[10] With the help and guidance of the Holy Spirit, the Church has developed the Rite of the Mass by which the Lord's Supper is continually renewed in every time and place. By the Rite of the Mass, we are united with our Lord in His Eucharistic Sacrifice. In the words of Pope Benedict XVI, we enter into the "hour"

---

[7] *Sacramentum Caritatis*, n. 9.
[8] *Sacramentum Caritatis*, n. 10.
[9] *Ibid.*
[10] *Sacramentum Caritatis*, n. 11.

of our Lord Jesus, that is, "[t]he Eucharist draws us into Jesus' act of self-oblation."[11] Uniting ourselves to our Lord Jesus, our lives are animated by the total outpouring of self in love. Our Holy Father reminds us that the changing of the bread and the wine into the Body and Blood of Christ in the Eucharistic Sacrifice is "a change meant to set off a process which transforms reality, a process leading ultimately to the transfiguration of the entire world, to the point where God will be all in all (cf. *1 Cor* 15:28)."[12]

Holy Eucharist, Work of the Holy Spirit

The Holy Spirit helps and guides the Church in developing the fitting liturgical rites by which the Eucharistic Sacrifice is celebrated down to our day. Our Holy Father tells us: "We need a renewed awareness of the decisive role played by the Holy Spirit in the evolution of the liturgical form and the deepening understanding of the sacred mysteries."[13] The Holy Spirit, Who was dwelling in all His fullness in our Lord Jesus, is poured forth by our Lord into the souls of His disciples, so that they may do all that our Lord asks of them. "Thus it is through the working of the Spirit that Christ himself continues to be present and active in his Church, starting with her vital center which is the Eucharist."[14]

In the Eucharistic Sacrifice, before the words of institution by which our Lord transforms the bread and wine into His true Body, Blood, Soul and Divinity, the priest calls down the Holy Spirit upon the gifts of bread and wine, so that God the Father may change them into the Body and Blood of

---

[11] *Deus Caritas Est*, n. 13.
[12] *Sacramentum Caritatis*, n. 11.
[13] *Sacramentum Caritatis*, n. 12.
[14] *Ibid*.

Christ, His Son and our Lord. The same Holy Spirit makes one the many members of the Body of Christ, uniting them in the outpouring of their lives, with Christ, for the sake of their brothers and sisters.[15]

Holy Eucharist, Birth and Life of the Church

The Church, the one Body of Christ, was born from the pierced side of Christ. From the pierced Heart of Jesus on the Cross, water and blood poured out, symbolizing the life of the Church, above all in the Sacraments of Baptism and the Holy Eucharist. As was just recalled, the Church is commanded by our Lord to celebrate the Holy Eucharist, but, at the same time, the Holy Eucharist gives birth to the Church and builds up the Church in unity and peace. In the relationship between the Church and the Holy Eucharist, we see that the celebration of the Holy Eucharist is only possible because Christ has first given Himself to us in the Eucharistic Sacrifice and Banquet. Our Holy Father observes that "the Church is able to celebrate and adore the mystery of Christ present in the Eucharist precisely because Christ first gave himself to her in the sacrifice of the Cross."[16] In the celebration of the Holy Eucharist, we understand the meaning of the words of Saint John in his First Letter: "We love, because he first loved us" (*1 Jn* 4:19).

The faithful are all one in the Church through the Holy Eucharist. Through the Holy Eucharist, we share in the communion of the Triune God, which is the source of our communion with each other. Pope Benedict XVI reminds us of the outstanding presentation of the mystery of the Holy Eucharist and communion in *Ecclesia de Eucharistia*.

---

[15] Cf. *Sacramentum Caritatis*, n. 13.
[16] *Sacramentum Caritatis*, n. 14.

Our Holy Father reflects on the individuation of each Christian community in the Eucharistic Sacrifice, which also, at the same time, makes each individual Christian community one with the Church universal. Our Holy Father comments: "From this Eucharistic perspective, adequately understood, ecclesial communion is seen to be catholic by its very nature."[17] The unity of each Christian community with the one Body of Christ throughout the whole world is reflected in a special way in the celebration of the Holy Mass by the Bishop, a successor to the Apostles, with the priests, his co-workers, and with the participation of all of the faithful.

Finally, in the discussion of the relationship of the Church and the Holy Eucharist, Pope Benedict XVI underlines the important contribution of Eucharistic faith and practice "to the ecumenical dialogue with the Churches and Ecclesial Communities which are not in full communion with the See of Peter."[18] Our Holy Father reminds us that the Holy Eucharist constitutes "a powerful bond of unity between the Catholic Church and the Orthodox Churches, which have preserved the authentic and integral nature of the Eucharistic Mystery."[19] He also notes that "the ecclesial character of the Eucharist can become an important element of the dialogue with the Communities of the Reformed tradition."[20]

The Holy Eucharist and the Other Sacraments

All of the Sacraments are essentially related to the Holy Eucharist, even as the whole of our Christian life has its

---

[17] *Sacramentum Caritatis*, n. 15.
[18] *Ibid.*
[19] *Ibid.*
[20] *Ibid.*

source in the Eucharistic Mystery and flows from our participation in the Eucharistic Sacrifice. Pope Benedict XVI observes that we can best understand the central place of the Holy Eucharist in the life of the Church by remembering that the Church herself is a sacrament in the sense that she is a visible and efficacious instrument of our communion with God and with all our brothers and sisters.[21] It is through the seven Sacraments that the Church is a sacrament. They are the privileged means by which Christ, alive in the Church, continues to pour out the Holy Spirit into our souls and to nourish and restore the life of the Holy Spirit dwelling within us. The Holy Father observes:

> The Church *receives* and at the same time *expresses* what she herself is in the seven Sacraments, thanks to which God's grace concretely influences the lives of the faithful, so that their whole existence, redeemed by Christ, can become an act of worship pleasing to God.[22]

---

[21] Cf. *Sacramentum Caritatis*, n. 16.
[22] *Ibid.*

- 9 -

The Holy Eucharist and the Sacraments of Initiation

There are three Sacraments by which we enter fully into the life of Christ: Baptism, Confirmation and the Holy Eucharist. For that reason, they are called the Sacraments of Christian Initiation. Pope Benedict XVI reminds us that Baptism and Confirmation are directed to the Holy Eucharist by which we have the fullness of communion with Christ in His Church. By Baptism, we are cleansed of original sin and brought to life in Christ and become members of His Mystical Body, the Church. Our baptismal entrance into the Church is brought to perfection with the reception of First Holy Communion. "The Holy Eucharist, then, brings Christian initiation to completion and represents the center and goal of all sacramental life."[1]

The Holy Father discusses the order in which the Sacraments of Initiation are received. In the Eastern Catholic Churches, the relationship of the Holy Eucharist, as the perfection of the gift of the Holy Spirit, which is given in Baptism and is strengthened and increased in Confirmation, is more clearly visible. The practice of the Eastern Churches is to confer the Sacrament of Confirmation immediately after baptism. In the Latin Church, the same order is followed

---

[1] *Sacramentum Caritatis*, n. 17.

when baptizing children who have reached the age of reason and when baptizing adults.

In the Latin Church, there is a diversity of practice in the case of those baptized as infants. In some dioceses, children who were baptized as infants are confirmed before making their First Holy Communion. In other dioceses, children are confirmed a little later, especially as they are entering into their adolescent years. Regarding the diversity of practice, the Holy Father reminds us that the order of reception of Confirmation and First Holy Communion is a question of good pastoral practice. It does not pertain to the doctrine of the faith. He concludes: "Concretely, it needs to be seen which practice better enables the faithful to put the Sacrament of the Eucharist at the center, as the goal of the whole process of initiation."[2]

Pope Benedict concludes the treatment of the relationship of the Holy Eucharist to Baptism and Confirmation by underlining the relationship of Christian initiation to the family and family life. He stresses the importance of the involvement of the family in the reception of the Sacraments of Baptism, Confirmation and the Holy Eucharist. In a particular way, he underlines the important role of the family at the time of the reception of First Holy Communion: "For many of the faithful, this day continues to be memorable as the moment when, even if in a rudimentary way, they first came to understand the importance of a personal encounter with Jesus."[3]

The Holy Father's words recalled to my mind the day of my reception of First Holy Communion. I remember so well the care with which my parents, my parish priests and the

---

[2] *Sacramentum Caritatis*, n. 18.
[3] *Sacramentum Caritatis*, n. 19.

religious Sisters at Saint Mary's School in Richland Center, Wisconsin, prepared me for the coming of our Eucharistic Lord into my soul. With a child's understanding, I knew that our Lord was with me in a new and most intimate way, a wonderful way in which He would continue to be with me throughout my lifetime. I can honestly say that the day of my First Holy Communion has been the point of reference for my whole life in the Church.

- IO -

The Holy Eucharist and the Sacraments of Healing

Penance

The more we appreciate the reality of the Holy Eucharist, the more we are led to confess our sins and receive our Lord's forgiveness in the Sacrament of Penance. The reality of the Blessed Sacrament requires that we be properly disposed to receive the Body and Blood of Christ. Our Holy Father reflects upon the diminished sense of sin in our highly secularized society and the consequent "superficiality in the understanding of God's love."[1] It is, therefore, important for the Church to pay attention to the "elements within the Rite of the Mass that express consciousness of personal sin and, at the same time, of God's mercy."[2] Reflecting upon the essential relationship between the Sacraments of the Holy Eucharist and Penance, we also become more conscious of the damage which our personal sins inflict upon the communion of the Church. Through the Sacrament of Penance, our communion with the Body of Christ is restored. The fullest expression of the restored communion is participation in the Eucharistic Sacrifice.

Regarding the relationship of the Holy Eucharist and

[1] *Sacramentum Caritatis*, n. 20.
[2] *Ibid.*

Penance, Pope Benedict XVI expresses several pastoral concerns, urging priests to "dedicate themselves with generosity, commitment and competency to administering the sacrament of Reconciliation."[3] He gives four practical directives.

First of all, confessionals in our churches are to be "clearly visible expressions of the importance of this sacrament."[4] Secondly, great care is to be exercised by the parish priests in the celebration of the Sacrament of Penance, keeping in mind that the individual confession of sins and individual absolution "is the only form intended for ordinary use."[5] Thirdly, the Holy Father asks that there be a priest with the responsibility of Penitentiary in every diocese to help meet "the need to rediscover sacramental forgiveness."[6] The Penitentiary holds a very important office in canon law, for he can absolve from many ecclesiastical penalties without recourse to higher authority.[7]

Lastly, Pope Benedict XVI stresses the important role of "a balanced and sound practice of gaining indulgences, whether for oneself or for the dead,"[8] in restoring the right understanding of the relationship of the Holy Eucharist and Penance. Although our sins are forgiven in the Sacrament of Penance, they involve a temporal punishment which needs to be remitted. Through the practice of indulgences, the Church draws upon the infinite merits of our Redeemer for the remission of the temporal punishment due to our sins and the sins of our deceased brothers and sisters with whom we are one in the Communion of the Saints. The seeking of

---

[3] *Sacramentum Caritatis*, n. 21.
[4] *Ibid.*
[5] *Ibid.*
[6] *Ibid.*
[7] Cf. Can. 508.
[8] *Sacramentum Caritatis*, n. 21.

indulgences expresses our deep consciousness "that by our own efforts alone we would be incapable of making reparation for the wrong we have done, and that the sins of each individual harm the whole community."[9] Our Holy Father reminds us that the very conditions for obtaining an indulgence, namely "going to confession and receiving sacramental communion," remind us of our constant need of conversion of life and of the "centrality of the Eucharist"[10] in our daily Christian living.

Anointing of the Sick

The reality of the Holy Eucharist is expressed in a particular way in the administration of the Sacrament of the Anointing of the Sick, for it "unites the sick with Christ's self-offering for the salvation of all, so that they, too, within the mystery of the communion of saints, can participate in the redemption of the world."[11] In a secularized society which views sickness and suffering as completely negative and meaningless, the Holy Eucharist reveals the mystery of love in the acceptance of suffering for the salvation of others. Even as the crucified Body of Christ, now gloriously seated at the right hand of the Father, is the greatest treasure of the Church, so also those who are sick and suffering are to be treasured by all in the Church and are a great source of blessing to all, when they embrace their suffering with and in Christ. The Sacrament of the Anointing of the Sick expresses the communion of our Lord with those who are seriously ill.[12]

---

[9] *Ibid.*
[10] *Ibid.*
[11] *Sacramentum Caritatis*, n. 22.
[12] Cf. *Ibid.*

Our Holy Father devotes special attention to Viaticum, the Holy Eucharist given to the dying, for it makes eloquently clear the relationship of the Holy Eucharist to the Anointing of the Sick. When we are dying, we most fully enter with Christ into the mystery of the Passover from this life to the eternal life which is to come. The Church fervently desires, therefore, that the dying be fortified with the Bread of Heaven, the Body and Blood of Christ. Regarding the administration of Holy Communion to the dying, Pope Benedict XVI declares: "On their journey to the Father, communion in the Body and Blood of Christ appears as the seed of eternal life and the power of the resurrection. . . . Since viaticum gives the sick a glimpse of the fullness of the Paschal Mystery, its administration should be readily provided for."[13] The fact that Holy Communion is an anticipation of the life to come also means that it commits us to preparing the day of Christ's final coming during each moment of our lives.

---

[13] *Ibid.*

an attitude of interior openness to a priestly calling."[6] In this regard, the Holy Father stresses the importance of vocational discernment, so that candidates admitted to studies for the priesthood will have the requisite qualities of a true shepherd of the flock. He notes, too, the discouragement and even scandal which a poorly formed clergy is for those whom Christ is calling to the priesthood.

The apostolate of priestly vocations is the responsibility of the whole Church and, as our Holy Father points out, needs to involve "every area of her life."[7] The family has a particular role in the apostolate of priestly vocations. Pope Benedict XVI expresses concern about families who "are often indifferent or even opposed to the idea of a priestly vocation."[8] In the family, children are brought up with respect for the gift of human life and for the Christian vocation to holiness, to doing God's will in all things. He reminds us that families "must have the courage to set before young people the radical decision to follow Christ, showing them how deeply rewarding it is."[9]

The Holy Father concludes the discussion of the shortage of priests by exhorting us to trust in the Providence of God Who always calls a sufficient number of men to serve His holy people in the ordained priesthood. At the same time, the Holy Father expresses "the gratitude of the whole Church for those bishops and priests who carry out their respective missions with fidelity, devotion and zeal."[10]

At the recommendation of the Synod of Bishops, the Holy Father noted with special gratitude the service of diocesan

---

[6] *Sacramentum Caritatis*, n. 25.
[7] *Ibid.*
[8] *Ibid.*
[9] *Ibid.*
[10] *Sacramentum Caritatis*, n. 26.

- II -

The Holy Eucharist and Holy Orders

The Holy Eucharist is the reason for the existence of the Sacrament of Holy Orders. At the Last Supper, our Lord Jesus both instituted the Holy Eucharist and consecrated the Apostles as priests for the offering of the Holy Eucharist. The priest is ordained to act in the person of Christ, the Shepherd and Head of the Father's flock. The priest acts in the person of Christ, Shepherd and Head, above all when he gives his hands and voice to Christ Who consecrates the bread and wine, changing them into His Body and Blood for our spiritual nourishment.

Pope Benedict XVI, inspired by the discussion of the Synod of Bishops, stresses several points regarding the relationship of the Holy Eucharist to Holy Orders. The first point is the truth that the relationship "is seen most clearly at Mass, when the Bishop or priest presides in the person of Christ the Head."[1] We understand best the vocation and mission of the priest and Bishop when we participate in Holy Mass at our parish church or at the cathedral church.

The celebration of the Chrism Mass on the morning of Holy Thursday is a most privileged occasion to witness the Bishop—and the priests in union with the Bishop—offering

---

[1] *Sacramentum Caritatis*, n. 23.

the Eucharistic Sacrifice for the whole flock. Fittingly, during the celebration of the Chrism Mass, the priests renew their commitment to priestly service, and the blessing of the holy oils and the consecration of the Sacred Chrism for use throughout the diocese takes place. The Bishop presides and as many of the priests as possible concelebrate with the Bishop. Even as the sacraments and sacramentals, in which the Holy Oils and Sacred Chrism are employed by the Bishop and the priests on our behalf, bring us the healing and strength of our Eucharistic Lord, so the Oils and Chrism are rightly set apart, blessed and consecrated within the solemn celebration of the Holy Eucharist in the cathedral church.

The priest, at the Holy Mass, not only acts in the person of Christ the Shepherd and Head of the flock, but he also acts in the name of the Church, offering to God the Father the most perfect prayer of all the faithful. "As a result, priests should be conscious of the fact that in their ministry they must never put themselves or their personal opinions in first place, but Jesus Christ." In all things and especially in the offering of the Eucharistic Sacrifice, the priest "must continually work at being a sign pointing to Christ, a docile instrument in the Lord's hands."[2]

The attentive care of the priest to celebrate the Rite of the Mass as the Church celebrates it, and without drawing any attention to his own person, manifests his vocation and mission on behalf of the flock he serves. Our Holy Father encourages priests "to see their eucharistic ministry as a humble service offered to Christ and his Church."[3]

---

[2] *Ibid.*
[3] *Ibid.*

The Holy Eucharist and Priestly Celibacy

Pope Benedict XVI reflects upon priestly celibacy as complete configuration to Christ in His self-offering on Calvary, the self-offering sacramentally renewed in the Holy Eucharist. The meaning of priestly celibacy is uncovered in the celibacy of Christ Who lived the mystery of His celibate love to the very outpouring of His life on the Cross. Priestly celibacy cannot be fully understood in "functional terms," but rather in terms of the union of the heart of the priest with the glorious pierced Heart of Jesus in love of the flock. The choice of priestly celibacy "has first and foremost a nuptial meaning; it is a profound identification with the heart of Christ the Bridegroom who gives his life for Bride."[4] Our Holy Father affirms that the priest's celibate love is "an immense blessing for the Church and for so itself."[5]

The Holy Eucharist and the Shortage of Priests

The discussion of the relationship of the Holy Eucharist Holy Orders naturally leads to the discussion of the of priests. Pope Benedict XVI, referring to the dis the subject at the Synod of Bishops, gives several First, he urges a constant attention to the proper of priests, in order that the Church responds throughout the world. Secondly, he recomme initiatives aimed at promoting, especially amo

---

[4] *Sacramentum Caritatis*, n. 24.
[5] *Ibid.*

priests in the missions, in response to the encyclical letter *Fidei Donum* of the Venerable Pope Pius XII, signed on April 21, 1957. He thanks God "for all those priests who have suffered even to the sacrifice of their lives in order to serve Christ."[11]

The Holy Eucharist and the Permanent Diaconate

The permanent deacons who are ordained "not for priest-hood but for service"[12] assist the bishops and priests by their ministry of proclaiming the Word of God, assisting at the altar and administering the Church's charitable works. Deacons are always united to the bishop and his priests and, therefore, serve by their teaching of Eucharistic faith and their promotion of Eucharistic life and devotion. Their service of the faithful is always carried out at the direction of the parish priest and the bishop.

---

[11] *Ibid.*
[12] *Ibid.*

The Holy Eucharist and the Sacrament of Holy Matrimony

The Holy Eucharist is rightly called a nuptial sacrament, for it is the highest expression of the love of Christ the Bridegroom for the Church, His Bride. In the Eucharistic Sacrifice, Christ gives His life, totally and forever, in love of the Church. It is Christ's love of all mankind which is sealed in the outpouring of His life on Calvary, the outpouring which the Holy Eucharist makes present in every time and place.[1] The love of husband and wife in marriage is a most special participation in the nuptial—that is, faithful and enduring—love of Christ for the Church and, indeed, for all mankind.

The Holy Eucharist sustains the unity and permanence of the love of man and woman in marriage. In the celebration of the Eucharistic Sacrifice, the married couple see the true and full image of the love to which they are called. Pope Benedict XVI makes reference to Saint Paul's teaching on married love:

> Indeed, in the theology of St. Paul, conjugal love is a sacramental sign of Christ's love for his Church, a love culminating in the Cross, the expression of His "marriage" with

---

[1] Cf. *Sacramentum Caritatis*, n. 27.

humanity and at the same time the origin and heart of the Eucharist.[2]

Reflecting on the relationship of the Holy Eucharist to Holy Matrimony, the Holy Father recalls that the family, formed by the union of man and woman in marriage, is the Church at home, the first place in which the life of the Church is realized and experienced. He also underlines "the unique mission of women in the family and in society, a mission that needs to be defended, protected and promoted."[3]

The Holy Eucharist and the Unicity of Marriage

"The indissoluble, exclusive and faithful bond uniting Christ and the Church, which finds sacramental expression in the Eucharist, corresponds to the basic anthropological fact that man is meant to be definitively united to one woman and vice versa."[4] In the context of the exclusive nature of marital love, reflected in the exclusive love of Christ for all mankind in the Holy Eucharist, Pope Benedict XVI addresses the pastoral approach to the practice of polygamy in some cultures. The Church, of course, can never bless a union which is not exclusive, that is, not between one man and one woman.

What about the situation of a person in polygamous relationships who is converted to the Catholic faith? Receiving the gift of faith, the person in question also receives the grace to conform his life to Christ. The Church accompanies the catechumen with compassion as he makes "whatever sac-

---

[2] *Ibid.*
[3] *Ibid.*
[4] *Sacramentum Caritatis*, n. 28.

rifices are necessary in order to arrive at perfect ecclesial communion."[5] Once the person has understood the mystery of Christ's love, expressed most perfectly in the Eucharistic Sacrifice, he will want to rectify his marital situation, in accord with the truth of marriage in Christ.

The Holy Eucharist and the Indissolubility of Marriage

In the context of discussing the indissolubility of marital love, Pope Benedict XVI addresses the painful situation of the divorced and remarried, which sadly is frequently repeated in a culture marked by a high percentage of marriages ending in divorce. The Synod of Bishops set forth again the Church's discipline, founded on the Word of God, which denies the sacraments to the divorced and remarried "since their state and their condition of life objectively contradict the loving union of Christ and the Church, signified and made present in the Eucharist."[6]

The Holy Father hastens to point out that the divorced and remarried, even though they may not receive the sacraments, remain members of the Church, encouraging them to participate in the Holy Mass without receiving Holy Communion, to take part in Eucharistic adoration, to engage in other forms of prayer, and to be active in the life of the parish. He also urges them to be in regular communication with their parish priest for spiritual assistance and to dedicate themselves to works of charity and penance and to the education of their children.

---

[5] *Ibid.*
[6] *Sacramentum Caritatis*, n. 29.

Regarding the situation of a divorced Catholic who believes that his or her marriage is null, that is, that it was not a true marriage from the beginning, Pope Benedict XVI comments on the need of a matrimonial tribunal in each diocese, which operates according to the norms of canon law in service of the truth about the marriage bond, in general and in the specific cases brought before it. As the Holy Father wisely observes, there can be no conflict between the pastoral care of the divorced and the requirements of the law, for both are to serve the truth which is at the foundation of every relationship of love. Repeating words spoken to the judges of the Roman Rota, which is his own chief matrimonial tribunal, the Holy Father declared that "it is a grave obligation to bring the Church's institutional activity in her tribunals ever closer to the faithful."[7]

If, in a particular case, the tribunal does not find for the nullity of the marriage and the parties involved cannot, for good reason, separate from each other, the couple is urged to live their relationship "in fidelity to the demands of God's law, as friends, as brother and sister,"[8] so that they may once again receive the Holy Eucharist. The decision to live in accord with God's law will require the knowledge and assistance of the parish priest. In accord with the Church's practice, all scandal must be avoided, and it must be clear that the relationship is not blessed by the Church as a marital relationship.

---

[7] Pope Benedict XVI, Address to the Tribunal of the Roman Rota for the Inauguration of the Judicial Year (January 28, 2006): *Acta Apostolicae Sedis* 98 (2006), 138, in *Sacramentum Caritatis*, n. 29.

[8] *Sacramentum Caritatis*, n. 29.

The Holy Eucharist and Preparation for Marriage

Pope Benedict XVI concludes the discussion of the relationship between the Holy Eucharist and Holy Matrimony by urging, in accord with the recommendation of the bishops at the Synod, "maximum pastoral attention to training couples preparing for marriage and to ascertaining beforehand their convictions regarding the obligations required for the validity of the sacrament of Matrimony."[9] The Holy Father calls for the Church's "full pastoral commitment"[10] to a fitting program of preparation for marriage, reminding us that a lack of care for marriage and the family is injurious to society itself.

Certainly, marriage preparation should lead young couples to recognize in the Holy Eucharist the source and highest expression of married love. The preparation of couples for marriage should, in every aspect, center upon the great mystery of Christ the Bridegroom's love of His Bride, the Church, the Mystery of Faith contained in the Holy Eucharist.

---

[9] *Ibid.*
[10] *Ibid.*

- 13 -

The Holy Eucharist and Eschatology

Eschatology is the name given to the study of our final destiny, what we have traditionally called the Last Things: Death, Judgment, the Resurrection of the Body, Heaven, Purgatory, and Hell. Clearly, the Holy Eucharist is essential to our pilgrimage to our lasting home with God in Heaven. Christ poured out His life on Calvary in His Sacrifice, which is made sacramentally present in every celebration of the Holy Mass, in order that we may enjoy eternal life with Him. The Holy Eucharist is the spiritual food of our earthly pilgrimage which reaches its completion in our passing from this life to the life which is to come. The Real Presence of Christ in the Most Blessed Sacrament permits us, already now, to share in the company of Christ, which we are destined to have with Him perfectly in Heaven.

In the Holy Eucharist, we recognize the immeasurable and totally selfless love of God Who desires that we share His friendship and company for all eternity. We know our sins and the ways in which we betray God's love in our daily living. In the Holy Eucharist, we receive the Heavenly Food which heals "our wounded freedom."[1] The Holy Eucharist nourishes the life of the Holy Spirit within us to free us

---

[1] *Sacramentum Caritatis*, n. 30.

from sin and to free us for the selfless love of God and our neighbor.

The Holy Eucharist opens up to us the deepest reality of our life on earth and of our world itself, namely, our destiny and our world's destiny in God, the destiny to be realized on the Last Day, when Christ returns in glory. Pope Benedict XVI reminds us that the Holy Eucharist guides us to our final destiny:

> Even though we remain "aliens and exiles" in this world (*1 Pet* 2:11), through faith we already share in the fullness of risen life. The Eucharistic Banquet, by disclosing its powerful eschatological dimension, comes to the aid of our freedom as we continue our journey.[2]

For us, it never makes sense "to live as if there were no tomorrow," for there is an eternal tomorrow which we experience each time we participate in the Holy Mass and pray in the presence of the Most Blessed Sacrament.

Inauguration of the Marriage Feast of the Lamb

At the Last Supper, our Lord Jesus inaugurated an event for which the People of Israel and, indeed, all of humanity and creation itself look with deepest desire: the fulfillment of God's promise to bring all mankind into one and to restore our world to the order with which He had created it. Pope Benedict XVI describes for us the eschatological meaning of Christ's calling of the Apostles and His consecration of them, at the Last Supper, to offer the Eucharistic Sacrifice:

> In the calling of the Twelve, which is to be understood in relation to the twelve tribes of Israel, and in the command

---

[2] *Ibid.*

he gave them at the Last Supper, before his redemptive Passion, to celebrate his memorial, Jesus showed that he wished to transfer to the entire community which he had founded the task of being, within history, the sign and instrument of the eschatological gathering that had its origin in him.[3]

Each time the Holy Mass is offered, all of mankind is gathered together by the love of Christ and is offered to God the Father, in anticipation of Christ's coming in glory at the end of time.

At the Holy Eucharist, our Lord gave to all His disciples the mission confided by God the Father to the Chosen People, the mission of bringing the Redeemer into the world. The Jewish people retain always the honor and dignity of being the first to be chosen by God as the messengers of His saving work through the coming of the Messiah, the Christ. But the Christ, now in the world, gives to all His disciples a share in the mission of evangelization, of announcing the Gospel to all the nations, of celebrating the Holy Eucharist in every time and place.

Offering Masses for the Dead

Reflecting upon the relationship of the Holy Eucharist to our final destiny and the final destiny of our world reminds us of the importance of praying for the dead and, above all, of having Masses offered for their eternal rest. Our love for our brothers and sisters who have died is expressed in our prayers for their final purification of all sin and their eternal joy and peace at the table of the "marriage supper

---

[3] *Sacramentum Caritatis*, n. 31.

of the Lamb," the "green pastures," the "still waters," the prepared "table," to which our Lord, the Good Shepherd, leads us throughout our earthly pilgrimage (*Ps* 23:2, 5 and *Rev* 19:9). The most loving prayer which we can offer for the dead is the Eucharistic Sacrifice. Through the offering of the Holy Mass for the dead, our deceased brothers and sisters are helped along the way of purification (Purgatory) to attain their final destiny, the Kingdom of Heaven.

Our prayers for the dead and our offering of the Mass for their eternal rest are also an expression of the hope which animates us all along the way of our earthly pilgrimage, that is, the hope of joining them once again in the Kingdom of Heaven. Our participation in the Holy Mass and our prayer before the Blessed Sacrament keep us strong throughout the pilgrimage, and keep before our eyes the goal toward which we strive with sure hope every day. When Christ comes on the Last Day, our bodies will be raised to share in the glory of His Risen Body, and all who have died in Christ will enjoy one another's company once again. Pope Benedict XVI declares: "The eucharistic celebration, in which we proclaim that Christ has died and risen, and will come again, is a pledge of the future glory in which our bodies too will be glorified."[4]

---

[4] *Sacramentum Caritatis*, n. 32.

- 14 -

The Holy Eucharist and the Blessed Virgin Mary

The source and highest expression of our Christian life in the worship of the Holy Eucharist naturally leads us to recognize with deepest devotion and love the Blessed Virgin Mary who is the first and best of us to live in Christ and to attain, with Him, our final destiny. In a wonderful way, Pope Benedict XVI relates our faith in the Holy Eucharist to our devotion to the Blessed Virgin Mary:

> Although we are still journeying towards the complete fulfillment of our hope, this does not mean that we cannot already gratefully acknowledge that God's gifts to us have found their perfect fulfillment in the Virgin Mary, Mother of God and our Mother. Mary's Assumption body and soul into heaven is for us a sign of sure hope, for it shows us, on our pilgrimage through time, the eschatological goal of which the sacrament of the Eucharist enables us even now to have a foretaste.[1]

The life of Mary is the pattern of our own life, receiving our Lord into our very being through the outpouring of the Holy Spirit and following Him faithfully on the way of the Cross, which leads us, body and soul, to eternal glory. As Pope Benedict XVI observes, the Assumption of the Blessed

---

[1] *Sacramentum Caritatis*, n. 33.

Virgin Mary uncovers for us our final destiny which we
anticipate at each Holy Mass.

Our Lord brought to fullness Mary's discipleship by as-
suming her, body and soul, into Heaven at her passing from
this life to the next. So, too, our Lord will bring our discipleship to fullness at the Resurrection on the Last Day. We
believe, as the Apostles' Creed puts it, "in the Holy Spirit,
the holy Catholic Church, the communion of saints, the forgiveness of sins, the resurrection of the body, and life everlasting." As we witness the offering of the glorious Body
and Blood of Christ for our salvation in the Holy Eucharist,
we understand that our own body is destined to share in
the glory of Christ Who is seated at the right hand of the
Father.

Our meditation upon the life of Christ in the life of the
Virgin Mary leads us always to the Holy Eucharist, for our
Blessed Mother is ever directing us to her Divine Son. In
the words of Blessed Pope John Paul II, our Blessed Mother
is the "woman of the Eucharist." I recall the words of his
Encyclical Letter *Ecclesia de Eucharistia*:

> In repeating what Christ did at the Last Supper in obe-
> dience to his command: "Do this in memory of me!", we
> also accept Mary's invitation to obey him without hesita-
> tion: "Do whatever he tells you" (*Jn* 2:5). With the same
> maternal concern which she showed at the wedding feast
> of Cana, Mary seems to say to us: "Do not waver; trust in
> the words of my Son. If he was able to change water into
> wine, he can also turn bread and wine into his body and
> blood, and through this mystery bestow on believers the
> living memorial of his passover, thus becoming 'the bread
> of life.'"[2]

---

[2] *Ecclesia de Eucharistia*, n. 54.

When we participate in the Eucharistic Sacrifice, our Blessed Mother is one with us, exemplifying faith in Christ and drawing us into ever deeper love of Christ.

The Annunciation and the Deposition from the Cross

Our Holy Father reflects upon the mystery of God's love for us, so wonderfully manifested in the mysteries of the life of the Virgin Mary, beginning with her Immaculate Conception. He declares: "From the Annunciation to Pentecost, Mary of Nazareth appears as someone whose freedom is completely open to God's will."[3] In a true sense, we may describe our entire life as the struggle to express our freedom in the faithful following of Christ, that is, in the doing of God's will, with and in Christ, in all things. Our whole life is the story of daily conversion to Christ, conversion from the enslavement to sin, which is, at the same time, conversion to the freedom which Christ alone gives us. The struggle reaches its highest expression in our union with Christ in His Eucharistic Sacrifice. In the Eucharistic Sacrifice, we are one with the source of our freedom, our Lord Jesus Christ, in His victory over sin and everlasting death.

Our Blessed Mother both teaches us the way of conversion to Christ, of abandoning ourselves to God's will, and, as a loving mother, intercedes constantly for us that we may have the grace to enter ever more deeply, in our thoughts, words and actions, into the mystery of Christ's Suffering, Dying and Rising from the Dead. Both by her example and through her intercession, she leads us to our Lord in the

---

[3] *Sacramentum Caritatis*, n. 33.

Holy Eucharist. Pope Benedict XVI describes Mary's way of life, which is also our way:

> A virgin attentive to God's Word, she lives in complete harmony with his will; she treasures in her heart the words that come to her from God and, piecing them together like a mosaic, she learns to understand them more deeply (cf. *Lk* 2:19, 51); Mary is the great Believer who places herself confidently in God's hands, abandoning herself to his will.[4]

In the mysteries of the life of Mary, which are all essentially mysteries of the life of Christ, we see how God calls us through the Sacraments, and most especially the Holy Eucharist, to share with Him in the work of salvation, in the work of preparing daily His Final Coming in glory.

The relationship of the Blessed Virgin Mary to the Holy Eucharist is seen, in a striking way, by placing side by side the Annunciation and the Deposition from the Cross. At the Annunciation, our Blessed Mother accepted her vocation and mission as Mother of God. Through her obedient response to the Announcement of the Archangel Gabriel, Mary received the Redeemer into her womb for the salvation of mankind. As the Creed says, God the Son "was conceived by the Holy Spirit and born of the Virgin Mary." At the Annunciation, Mary emptied herself of her own will in order to make God's will her own.

Mary, Mother of Christ, continued to empty herself of her own will in doing God's will by becoming her Divine Son's most faithful disciple. She was one with Him throughout His public ministry. Her faithful and altogether excellent discipleship reached its height as she stood at the foot of the Cross upon which her Divine Son poured out His life for

---

[4] *Ibid.*

our eternal salvation and as she received His dead Body into her arms after he had been taken down from the Cross. Our Holy Father comments on the relationship of the Annunciation to the Deposition: "From the Annunciation to the Cross, Mary is the one who received the Word, made flesh within her and then silenced in death. It is she, lastly, who took into her arms the lifeless body of the one who truly loved his own 'to the end' (*Jn* 13:1)."[5]

The Blessed Virgin shared in a most privileged way in the saving work of Christ. She shows us how we are called to share, with and in Christ, in the salvation of the world. As our Lord was dying on the Cross, He gave His Mother to His Apostle John who represents us all in the Church. Mary, the Mother of Christ, is the Mother of the Church who lovingly leads her children to salvation in Christ, above all through the Sacrament of the Holy Eucharist.

Conclusion of Part One, A Mystery to Be Believed

Having completed our reflection on Part One of *Sacramentum Caritatis*, which treats faith in the Holy Eucharist, we are ready now to begin our reflection on Part Two which treats the celebration of the Holy Eucharist. Our study of Catholic faith in the Holy Eucharist is the essential preparation for our study of how the Church celebrates the Most Blessed Sacrament.

---

[5] *Ibid.*

Beauty and the Celebration
of the Sacred Liturgy

Part Two of *Sacramentum Caritatis*, which is entitled "The
Eucharist, a Mystery to Be Celebrated," examines the many
aspects of the celebration of the Mystery of Faith, especially
as they relate to the truth of the Most Blessed Sacrament.
The Holy Father begins Part Two by treating the essential
relationship between the law of praying and worshiping (*lex
orandi*) and the law of believing (*lex credendi*). Clearly, the
law of praying and worshiping holds always the first place
in the life of faith, for it is directed to the very experience
of the Mystery of Faith; it is the personal participation in
the saving action of the glorious Christ seated at the right
hand of the Father.

Pope Benedict XVI makes two points regarding the relationship of worship and faith, which must always be kept
in mind. First of all, "[t]heological reflection in this area
can never prescind from the sacramental order instituted by
Christ himself."[1] Secondly, "the liturgical action can never
be considered generically, prescinding from the mystery of
faith."[2] Without attention to the primary place of the liturgical action, the doctrine of the faith would be unnaturally

---

[1] *Sacramentum Caritatis*, n. 34.
[2] *Ibid.*

divorced from the personal, sacramental encounter with Christ which is the source of Catholic faith and its highest expression. At the same time, if the liturgical action is not understood through the eyes of Catholic faith, it risks being seen as a merely human ritual and, thereby, emptied of its deepest significance. Pope Benedict XVI declares: "Our faith and the eucharistic liturgy both have their source in the same event: Christ's gift of himself in the Paschal Mystery."[3]

The Sacred Liturgy and Beauty

The relationship of faith and worship is seen, in a particular way, in the beauty which is characteristic of both the Catholic faith and Catholic worship. There can be nothing more beautiful, more splendid, than the encounter with God the Son Incarnate in the Eucharistic Sacrifice, for the Holy Eucharist is the fullest expression of God's love of us. The encounter, as with all things truly beautiful, attracts us and frees us from the enslavements which keep us from following faithfully our vocation of pure and selfless love. The encounter frees us from all that would mar our beauty as true sons and daughters of God in God the Son. When we meet our Lord in the Holy Eucharist, we meet "beauty and splendor at their source."[4]

The Holy Father reflects on how God's beauty was first revealed by Him in the created world, and then in the wonderful deeds which He accomplished on behalf of His people in the Old Testament. The fullness of divine beauty was revealed in the coming of God the Son into the world in our

---

[3] *Ibid.*
[4] *Sacramentum Caritatis*, n. 35.

human flesh. "Christ is the full manifestation of the glory of God."[5]

The beauty of God is seen in Christ, not simply in His natural attractiveness but ultimately in His loss of all earthly attractiveness by His cruel Passion and Death. The glory of the Resurrection, the eternal splendor of the Risen Christ, comes by way of His Crucifixion and Death. Christ's glorious wounds are the fullest manifestation of His unsurpassable beauty, the beauty of unconditional love poured out "to the end" (*Jn* 13:1). "Here the splendor of God's glory surpasses all worldly beauty. The truest beauty is the love of God, who definitively revealed himself to us in the paschal mystery."[6]

The Sacred Liturgy, which makes always present for us the Paschal Mystery, is therefore a most privileged expression of divine beauty. It is "a glimpse of heaven on earth." The beauty of the Sacred Liturgy is the glorious Christ pouring out His life for our eternal salvation. Our attention to the fittingness and beauty of the various aspects of the Sacred Liturgy is directed to the great manifestation of God Himself in our Lord Jesus Christ, giving Himself to us with unconditional love.

Regarding the beauty of the Sacred Liturgy, Pope Benedict XVI concludes: "These considerations should make us realize the care which is needed, if the liturgical action is to reflect its innate splendor."[7] In preparing for the celebration of the Holy Eucharist and in the celebration itself, we must avoid anything careless, routine, improvised or stingy.

---

[5] *Ibid.*
[6] *Ibid.*
[7] *Ibid.*

The Sacred Liturgy, the Work of Christ

Christ Himself is at work in the Sacred Liturgy and, therefore, the celebration of the liturgy is beautiful in itself. The
whole Christ is at work in the Sacred Liturgy, that is, Christ,
the Head of His Mystical Body, and Christ in His Mystical
Body, the Church. Regarding the "profound unity between
ourselves and the Lord Jesus"[8] in the Holy Eucharist, Pope
Benedict quotes a passage from one of his favorite theologians, Saint Augustine of Hippo. Saint Augustine, in a sermon preached to the newly baptized on Easter Sunday in
the year 414 or 415, declares:

> The bread you see on the altar, sanctified by the word of
> God, is the body of Christ. The chalice, or rather, what
> the chalice contains, sanctified by the word of God, is the
> blood of Christ. In these signs, Christ the Lord willed to
> entrust to us his body and the blood which he shed for the
> forgiveness of our sins. If you have received them properly,
> you yourselves are what you have received.[9]

Through the Eucharistic Sacrifice, Christ makes ever
present the offering of His life for us and makes us one
with Him in offering our lives for our brothers and sisters.

The Holy Eucharist is the action of God, "which draws
us into Christ through the Holy Spirit."[10] The Eucharistic
Sacrifice, in its essential elements, remains always the same.
It is not subject to changes which we wish to introduce or
which are dictated by "the latest trends." Pope Benedict XVI

---

[8] *Sacramentum Caritatis*, n. 36.
[9] Saint Augustine of Hippo, *Sermo* 227, 1: *Patrologia Latina* 38, 1099, in
Sacramentum Caritatis, n. 36.
[10] *Sacramentum Caritatis*, n. 37.

reminds us of the words of Saint Paul regarding the celebration of the Holy Eucharist. Saint Paul makes it clear that he is handing on not his own creation or invention, but what he received from the Apostles who received it from our Lord Himself.

The Church celebrates the Holy Mass in virtue of our Lord's command at the Last Supper. The Apostles came to understand the command as they met our Risen Lord in the forty days after His Resurrection and before His Ascension, and as they were inspired by the Holy Spirit, poured out upon the Church on Pentecost Sunday. The Lord's command is fulfilled, above all, at Sunday Mass. "Sunday, the day Christ rose from the dead, is also the first day of the week, the day which the Old Testament tradition saw as the beginning of God's work of creation. The day of creation has now become the day of the 'new creation,' the day of our liberation, when we commemorate Christ who died and rose again."[11]

The Art of Proper Celebration

Pope Benedict XVI points out that the Bishops at the Synod had frequently insisted upon the relationship between the proper celebration of the Holy Eucharist and "the full, active and fruitful participation of all the faithful."[12] The Holy Father declares: "The primary way to foster the participation of the People of God in the sacred rite is the proper celebration of the rite itself."[13] What is the art of celebration? It "is the fruit of faithful adherence to the liturgical norms in all

---

[11] *Ibid.*
[12] *Sacramentum Caritatis*, n. 38.
[13] *Ibid.*

their richness; indeed, for two thousand years this way of celebrating has sustained the faith life of all believers, called to take part in the celebration as the People of God, a royal priesthood, a holy nation."[14]

The art of celebrating necessarily depends upon the discipline of the Bishop, priests and deacons who, according to their individual order, celebrate the Sacred Liturgy "as their principal duty."[15] The Diocesan Bishop has the first and most weighty responsibility for the right celebration of the Sacred Liturgy. The Diocesan Bishop has the responsibility for the correct ordering of the liturgical celebrations in every part of his diocese.

Only those liturgies celebrated in communion with the Diocesan Bishop are lawful in the diocese. In order to carry out his responsibility for the celebration of the Sacred Liturgy, the Diocesan Bishop must take care to deepen the understanding of the Holy Eucharist among all of the faithful, so that they may "thereby be led to an active and fruitful celebration of the Eucharist."[16] Given the responsibility of the Diocesan Bishop, Pope Benedict XVI asks "that every effort be made to ensure that the liturgies which the Bishop celebrates in his Cathedral" respect fully the liturgical norms, "so that they can be considered an example for the entire Diocese."[17]

---

[14] *Ibid.*

[15] *Sacramentum Caritatis*, n. 39.

[16] *General Instruction of the Roman Missal*, 22, in *Sacramentum Caritatis*, n. 39.

[17] *Sacramentum Caritatis*, n. 39.

Liturgical Norms,
Sacred Architecture and Art

The harmony in the celebration of the Sacred Liturgy is fostered and safeguarded by the liturgical norms which all are obliged to observe. These norms, which pertain to the rite itself, to the liturgical vestments, vessels and linens, and to the church and its furnishings, all serve the beauty of the rite which points to Christ, the all-beautiful One acting in the rite.

Pope Benedict XVI also indicates the importance of careful attention "to the various kinds of language that the liturgy employs: words and music, gestures and silence, movement, the liturgical colors of the vestments."[18] The creativity required by the art of celebrating has nothing to do with *ad hoc* innovations or with the totally false notion of making the Sacred Liturgy interesting, as if it were not in itself totally attractive. It consists, rather, in the attention to the rite itself and to the integrity of the individual elements of the rite, all of which point to the great gift of the Holy Eucharist and all of which invite the minister of the Holy Eucharist to have "a docile openness to receiving this ineffable gift."[19]

The innate beauty of the Sacred Liturgy demands special attention to the works of art, which serve the act of worship. The architecture of the church or chapel, in which the Sacred Liturgy is celebrated, "should highlight the unity of the furnishings of the sanctuary, such as the altar, the crucifix, the tabernacle, the ambo and the celebrant's chair."[20]

---

[18] *Sacramentum Caritatis*, n. 40.
[19] *Ibid.*
[20] *Sacramentum Caritatis*, n. 41.

The architecture of a church or chapel must be truly sacred, that is, "a fitting space for the celebration of the mysteries of the faith, especially the Eucharist."[21] Sacred architecture should assist the faithful gathered for worship to recognize their own identity as the "living stones of the Church" (cf. *1 Pet* 2:5).[22]

The sacred art employed in the Church should be directed to a deeper understanding of the sacraments as the privileged means by which Christ pours forth the grace of the Holy Spirit into our souls. Since priests have the responsibility for the choice and disposition of sacred art in our churches and chapels, Pope Benedict XVI reminds us that "it is essential that the education of seminarians and priests include the study of art history, with special reference to sacred buildings and the corresponding liturgical norms."[23] Everything which is at the service of the Eucharistic Sacrifice "should be marked by beauty."[24] Closely connected to the beauty of the sacred art, the paintings and sculptures and stained glass, is the beauty of the vestments, the vessels and the furniture, which should "foster awe for the mystery of God, manifest the unity of faith and strengthen devotion."[25]

Sacred Music

Sacred music has always had a most important part to play in the Church's worship. Pope Benedict XVI, once again, quotes Saint Augustine who rightly observes that "the new

[21] *Ibid.*
[22] *Ibid.*
[23] *Ibid.*
[24] *Ibid.*
[25] *Ibid.*

man sings a new song," the song of God's immeasurable love of us in Jesus Christ and our love of God, in return. Down the Christian centuries, the Church has developed a rich patrimony of music composed for the Sacred Liturgy, composed to lift up our minds and hearts to the great Mystery of Faith. "This heritage must not be lost."[26]

Regarding the music employed in the celebration of the Sacred Liturgy, our Holy Father notes that "one song is not as good as another."[27] Care must be taken so that the music, both in its form and content, respects the sublime reality of the Sacred Liturgy. Sacred music must be at the service of the liturgical celebration and, therefore, must be "well integrated into the overall celebration."[28] "Consequently everything—texts, music, execution—ought to correspond to the meaning of the mystery being celebrated, the structure of the rite and the liturgical seasons."[29]

Finally, an altogether special esteem must be shown toward Gregorian Chant, which is the form of music composed exclusively for sacred worship. Gregorian Chant is, of course, the greatest jewel in the body of music written specifically for the celebration of the Holy Mass. It is sacred music *par excellence*. Pope Benedict XVI notes that, "while respecting various styles and different and highly praiseworthy traditions," he, "in accordance with the request advanced by the Synod Fathers," desires "that Gregorian chant be suitably esteemed and employed as the chant proper to the Roman liturgy."[30]

---

[26] *Sacramentum Caritatis*, n. 42.
[27] *Ibid.*
[28] *Ibid.*
[29] *Ibid.*
[30] *Ibid.*

- 16 -

The Structure of the Eucharistic Celebration

Having treated the essential elements of the art of celebrating the Holy Eucharist (*ars celebrandi*), Pope Benedict XVI next takes up the discussion of the structure of the celebration of the Holy Mass, in the particular light of the implementation of the reforms mandated by the Second Vatican Ecumenical Council. He reminds us of the importance of a faithful implementation of the reforms mandated by the Council, which are set within the "great ecclesial tradition."[1]

The offering of the Holy Mass remains always the same in the living tradition of the Church, while reforms in the Rite of the Holy Mass may be made from time to time. Whatever those reforms may be, they must always relate to the celebration of the Holy Mass as the Church has faithfully handed it down in obedience to the mandate of our Lord at the Last Supper: "Do this in remembrance of me" (*1 Cor* 11:24–25).

The Rite of the Mass is divided into two principal parts: the Liturgy of the Word and the Liturgy of the Eucharist. Before entering into the discussion of each part, our Holy Father reminds us that the two parts are inherently related

---

[1] *Sacramentum Caritatis*, n. 43.

to each other in the one Rite of the Mass. Both the treatment of the Holy Mass in the teaching of the faith and the actual celebration of the Holy Mass must "avoid giving the impression that the two parts of the rite are merely juxtaposed."[2] Together with the introductory and concluding rites, the Liturgy of the Word and the Liturgy of the Eucharist constitute our integral and, in fact, highest act of worship of God.

It is through the hearing of the proclamation of the Word of God that our faith is informed for the Eucharistic Sacrifice. At the same time, hearing the Word of God stirs up in us the desire to be united with Our Lord Jesus Christ, the Word made flesh, in the Holy Eucharist. If we are to receive our Lord with faith and love in the Liturgy of the Eucharist, then we must nourish our minds and hearts by listening attentively to the Word of God as it is proclaimed and expounded for us in the Liturgy of the Word. Our Holy Father counsels us to keep in mind "that the word of God, read and proclaimed by the Church in the liturgy, leads to the Eucharist as to its own connatural end."[3]

The Liturgy of the Word

In taking up the discussion of the Liturgy of the Word, Pope Benedict XVI tells us that the Synod of Bishops wished to underline the importance of its careful preparation and celebration. The Holy Father, for his part, immediately urges "that every effort be made to ensure that the liturgical proclamation of the word of God is entrusted to well-prepared read-

---

[2] *Sacramentum Caritatis*, n. 44.
[3] *Ibid.*

ers."[4] Regarding the proclamation of the Readings and the Gospel, it is important that we keep in mind that God Himself speaks to us through the divinely inspired words of the Holy Scriptures. With what care and reverence, therefore, lectors or readers should carry out their service within the celebration of the Sacred Liturgy! In a most special way, Christ speaks to us in the Gospel, which, therefore, may only be proclaimed by an ordained minister, that is, deacon, priest or bishop.

At the same time, the Word of God "must be listened to and accepted in a spirit of communion with the Church and with a clear awareness of its unity with the Sacrament of the Eucharist."[5] To aid in the reception of the Word of God, the Holy Father notes that some introduction can be made to the readings, "in order to focus the attention of the faithful."[6] In any case, the hearer of the Word of God must always remember that all of the Holy Scriptures only find their full meaning in the person of Christ, Who remains always present for us in the Holy Eucharist. As a result, the more we hear the Word of God proclaimed and enter into a deeper understanding of the Holy Scriptures, the more we will comprehend and love the mystery of the Holy Eucharist.

To foster the more efficacious hearing of the Word of God proclaimed in the celebration of the Holy Eucharist, our Holy Father encourages other celebrations centered upon the proclamation and exposition of the Holy Scriptures, and the reading of the Holy Scriptures "in the context of prayer (*lectio divina*)."[7] To the same end, he encourages the praying

---

[4] *Sacramentum Caritatis*, n. 45.
[5] *Ibid.*
[6] *Ibid.*
[7] *Ibid.*

of the Liturgy of the Hours and the keeping of vigils by the faithful. "By praying the Psalms, the Scripture readings and the readings from the great tradition which are included in the Divine Office, we can come to a deeper experience of the Christ-event and the economy of salvation, which in turn can enrich our understanding and participation in the celebration of the Eucharist."[8]

The Homily

Fittingly, our Holy Father gives special attention to the homily within the Liturgy of the Word. He begins with the declaration: "Given the importance of the word of God, the quality of homilies needs to be improved."[9] The homily is integral to the celebration of the Holy Eucharist, for it helps the faithful to apply the Word of God to their daily living.

In order that the homily achieve its important purpose within the Sacred Liturgy and for the daily life of the faithful, the Holy Father asks those who preach to apply the proclaimed Word "to the sacramental celebration and the life of the community, so that the word of God truly becomes the Church's vital nourishment and support."[10] The homily should be catechetical and exhortative.

In order that the homilies, over a certain period of time, present the complete content of the Catholic faith and urge the faithful to put the complete faith into practice, Pope Benedict XVI suggests the fittingness of planning homilies, with attention to the readings and Gospel of each Sunday, so that all of the "great themes of the Christian faith" are

---

[8] *Ibid.*
[9] *Sacramentum Caritatis*, n. 46.
[10] *Ibid.*

treated within a certain period of time. He suggests as a guide in planning homilies what are called the four "pillars" of the *Catechism of the Catholic Church*: "the profession of faith, the celebration of the Christian mystery, life in Christ and Christian prayer."[11]

Presentation of the Gifts

The Presentation of the Gifts expresses symbolically the offering of the whole of creation for transformation, that is, salvation, by our Lord Jesus Christ. The simple elements of bread and wine, representing all of created reality, are presented so that the order which God the Father intended from the beginning of Creation might be restored by the Sacrifice of Christ. Since the coming of God the Son in our human flesh and His great work of salvation, all of creation awaits the day of Christ's Second Coming, when He will restore all things to the Father.

At the Presentation of the Gifts, we offer to our Lord all our sorrows and sufferings and those of our brothers and sisters throughout the world. Our Holy Father observes how the gesture involved points to the redemptive meaning of human suffering when it is united to the sufferings of Christ.

The significance of the Presentation of the Gifts "can be expressed without the need for undue emphasis or complexity."[12] The simplicity and directness of the action draws our attention to the call which God gives to each of us to participate in His only-begotten Son's saving work by uniting all we have and are, and in a special way our sorrows and sufferings, to the Passion and Death of Christ. Through the

---

[11] *Ibid.*

[12] *Sacramentum Caritatis*, n. 47.

Presentation of the Gifts, we are reminded of the dignity of our human labors, when we carry them out in Christ and with the help of His grace.

The Eucharistic Prayer

Quoting the *General Instruction of the Roman Missal*, our Holy Father enunciates the central and most elevated place of the Eucharistic Prayer in the whole structure of the celebration of the Holy Mass: "The Eucharistic Prayer is the 'center and summit of the entire celebration.' Its importance deserves to be adequately emphasized."[13]

The variety of Eucharistic Prayers reflects the great richness of the Church's Tradition as it hands down, from generation to generation, the Church's greatest treasure, the Body and Blood of Christ.

Drawing again upon the *General Instruction of the Roman Missal*, Pope Benedict XVI lists eight "basic elements of every Eucharistic Prayer: thanksgiving, acclamation, epiclesis, institution narrative and consecration, anamnesis, offering, intercessions and final doxology."[14] The epiclesis is the priest's calling down of the Holy Spirit for the consecration of the bread and wine. It takes place right before the institution narrative containing the words of the Consecration.

In an earlier part of *Sacramentum Caritatis*, our Holy Father noted the particular enrichment to our spiritual life which comes from appreciating the relationship between the calling-down of the Holy Spirit in the epiclesis and the words of Christ by which the bread and wine are changed

---

[13] *Sacramentum Caritatis*, n. 48.
[14] *Ibid.*

into His Body and Blood.[15] Once again, our Holy Father draws our attention to "the profound unity between the invocation of the Holy Spirit and the institution narrative."[16] At the epiclesis, the Church prays for the outpouring of the Holy Spirit, in order that the elements of bread and wine may be changed into the Body and Blood of Christ, and the faithful who receive the Body and Blood of Christ may be transformed more and more into Christ's likeness.

The Sign of Peace

Our Holy Father comments on the Eucharistic Sacrifice as the source of our peace and on the deep feeling surrounding this aspect of the Holy Eucharist in a world "fraught with fear and conflict."[17] Here, it is important to remember the Church's grave responsibility "to pray insistently for the gift of peace and unity for herself and for the whole human family."[18] The Sign of Peace has great significance within the Rite of the Mass, a significance which is understood with special intensity in our time.

The difficulty with the Sign of Peace, which the Synod of Bishops confronted, is the exaggeration of the manner of its exchange to the point of distracting seriously from the sacred moment of Holy Communion, the culmination of the Eucharistic Sacrifice. What must be recalled is that the Sign of Peace comes from Christ, Who is truly present on the Altar of Sacrifice. It is the Peace which is Christ's gift to us through His Passion, Death and Resurrection.

---

[15] Cf. *Sacramentum Caritatis*, n. 13.
[16] *Sacramentum Caritatis*, n. 48.
[17] *Sacramentum Caritatis*, n. 49.
[18] *Ibid.*

The Sign of Peace should be exchanged with profound respect for its deepest significance. The Sign of Peace is neither for visiting with one's neighbors nor for offering overly demonstrative signs of affection. "It should be kept in mind that nothing is lost when the sign of peace is marked by a sobriety which preserves the proper spirit of the celebration, as, for example, when it is restricted to one's immediate neighbors."[19]

Distribution and Reception of Holy Communion

The distribution and reception of Holy Communion mark the high point of the Eucharistic Sacrifice, the moment when the Consecration of the Body and Blood of Christ attains its proper end, that is, the Sacred Host and Precious Blood are reverently received and consumed by the faithful. Holy Communion is the most deeply personal moment of meeting our Lord on this earth. Given the singular importance of Holy Communion, Pope Benedict XVI issues an appeal regarding the distribution of Holy Communion: "I ask everyone, especially ordained ministers and those who, after adequate preparation and in cases of genuine need, are authorized to exercise the ministry of distributing the Eucharist, to make every effort to ensure that this simple act preserves its importance as a personal encounter with the Lord Jesus in the sacrament."[20] Specifically, Pope Benedict XVI has asked that the recently issued norms and directives in the matter be carefully followed. "All Christian

---

· [19] *Ibid.*
[20] *Sacramentum Caritatis*, n. 50.

communities are to observe the current norms faithfully, seeing in them an expression of the faith and love with which we all must regard this sublime sacrament."[21]

Our Holy Father also asks that a time of silence be observed after Holy Communion, so that the communicant can offer thanksgiving to God for the greatest gift which He gives to us in the Church. The singing of a hymn during the Communion Rite is certainly appropriate, but respect must also be shown for the need of silence and silent prayer before the great mystery of God's love experienced in Holy Communion.

Our Holy Father addresses a "frequently encountered" pastoral difficulty, namely, "the fact that on certain occasions—for example, wedding Masses, funerals and the like —in addition to practicing Catholics there may be others present who have long since ceased to attend Mass or are living in a situation which does not permit them to receive the sacraments."[22] He also mentions the situation of "members of other Christian confessions and even other religions" who may be present at the Holy Eucharist. Pope Benedict XVI asks that we find "a brief and clear way to remind those present of the meaning of sacramental communion and the conditions required for its reception."[23] In a totally secularized and secularizing world, there is a great need for all to pay careful attention to the reality of the Holy Eucharist, as Saint Paul had already urged the faithful at Corinth in the early years of the Church's life (cf. *1 Cor* 11:27–29). Receiving Holy Communion is not some merely fraternal

---

[21] *Ibid.*
[22] *Ibid.*
[23] *Ibid.*

action of all present at Mass or a right which comes with presence at the Holy Mass. It is, rather, receiving the Body and Blood of Christ, for which one must be properly disposed.

Finally, our Holy Father reminds us that, if the circumstances of a situation "make it impossible to ensure that the meaning of the Eucharist is duly appreciated," then we should appropriately replace "the celebration of the Mass with a celebration of the word of God."[24] In other words, in a situation in which the greater part of those present cannot participate fully in the Holy Eucharist, it would be more appropriate simply to have a Liturgy of the Word together with prayer in common.

Conclusion: *Ite, Missa Est*

Pope Benedict XVI concludes his treatment of the structure of the Rite of the Mass by reminding us of the significance which the words of the dismissal have for our daily living. While the Latin word, *"missa,"* has a sense of dismissal, in the Church, at the conclusion of the Mass, it has come to refer to the mission of bringing Christ to the world. Our Holy Father asks that the faithful "be helped to understand more clearly this essential dimension of the Church's life, taking the dismissal as a starting-point."[25] He also asks that the texts of the Prayer over the People and the Final Blessing be enriched to make clear the essential connection between participation in the Holy Eucharist and active engagement in the mission of the Church.

[24] *Ibid.*
[25] *Sacramentum Caritatis*, n. 51.

Active, Full, and
Fruitful Participation

Continuing his treatment of the celebration of the Eucharistic Mystery in *Sacramentum Caritatis*, Pope Benedict XVI takes up the discussion of the qualities of the participation of the faithful in the Eucharistic Sacrifice. He reminds us of the call of the Second Vatican Ecumenical Council for "active, full and fruitful participation." He notes that "considerable progress"[1] has been made in responding to the Council's desire regarding the liturgical participation of the faithful.

The Holy Father also notes a certain failure to understand accurately what the Council intended by participation. The misunderstanding centers around the meaning of the Latin word *actuosa*, an adjective used to describe the desired participation of the faithful. The Latin word is usually translated by the English word "active," but it does not mean "mere external activity during the celebration."[2] It means, rather, a deeply interiorized participation, that is, participation in the sacred action of the Mass with awareness of its profound significance for our daily living. In other words, when we participate in the Holy Mass, we are not onlookers. We are

---

[1] *Sacramentum Caritatis*, n. 52.
[2] *Ibid.*

engaged in the action of Christ and are conscious of what our engagement means in terms of a life poured out in love of God and neighbor.[3]

The Holy Father lists some of the aspects of the participation of the faithful in Holy Mass, as they are set forth by the Second Vatican Ecumenical Council. These aspects include instruction through the proclamation and exposition of the Word of God, reception of the Body of Christ, the act of thanksgiving to God, and union with the priest in offering ourselves, with Christ, to God the Father, "not only through the hands of the priest but also together with him."[4]

Participation and the Service of the Priest, Deacon, and Liturgical Ministers

Active participation in the Eucharistic Sacrifice is fostered by a good understanding of the distinct functions of the faithful in the Sacred Liturgy. In particular, the distinct service of the priest must be understood. The priest "alone, and no other, as the tradition of the Church attests, presides over the entire Eucharistic celebration, from the initial greeting to the final blessing."[5] Configured to the person of Christ, Head and Shepherd of the flock, the priest most fully expresses his identity when he gives his whole being to Christ for the offering of the Mass. The ordained priest acts in the person of Christ in offering the Eucharistic Sacrifice, or, in other words, Christ acts.

The Holy Father reminds us that every celebration of the Holy Mass is led by the Bishop, chief shepherd of the flock,

---

[3] Cf. *Ibid.*
[4] *Ibid.*
[5] *Sacramentum Caritatis*, n. 53.

either by the Bishop himself or by a priest, a co-worker of the Bishop.[6] The unity of the Church throughout the world is experienced at every offering of the Mass through the one ministry of the Apostles and their successors, the Bishops, in communion with the Apostle Peter, head of the Apostles, and his successor, the Roman Pontiff.

The deacon also carries out a distinctive service during the Eucharistic Liturgy, which should not be confused with the other liturgical ministries. The deacon "prepares the altar, assists the priest, proclaims the Gospel, preaches the homily from time to time, reads the intentions of the Prayer of the Faithful, and distributes the Eucharist to the faithful."[7]

The Holy Father also makes reference to the liturgical ministries "which can be carried out in a praiseworthy manner by religious and properly trained laity."[8] In a footnote, Pope Benedict XVI quotes one of the conclusions of the Synod of Bishops, which recalls to our minds that such ministries "must be introduced in accordance with the real needs of the celebrating community"; that those appointed to the ministries must be "chosen with care, well prepared, and provided with ongoing formation"; that their appointment is for a defined time; and, finally, that they "must be known to the community and be gratefully acknowledged by the community."[9] Some examples of liturgical ministers are lectors (readers), cantors and extraordinary ministers of Holy Communion.

---

[6] Cf. *Ibid.*

[7] *Ibid.*

[8] *Ibid.*

[9] *Sacramentum Caritatis*, note 162.

Inculturation

Pope Benedict XVI next takes up the discussion of "adaptations appropriate to different contexts and cultures,"[10] which promote participation in the Sacred Liturgy. While the Holy Father acknowledges that "certain abuses have occurred" in carrying out inculturation, he stresses that the "clear principle" of inculturation "must be upheld in accordance with the real needs of the Church as she lives and celebrates the mystery of Christ in a variety of cultural situations."[11] God became man, the Second Person of the Most Holy Trinity took our human flesh, in order to fulfill His desire "to encounter us in our own concrete situation."[12] Inculturation must always be understood and carried out in the light of the mystery of the Incarnation.

Pope Benedict XVI notes that the "possibilities" of inculturation are defined in the General Instruction of the Roman Missal, in the directives of the Congregation for Divine Worship and the Discipline of the Sacraments, and in Blessed Pope John Paul II's post-synodal apostolic exhortations for Africa, America, Asia, Europe and Oceania. It is the Conference of Bishops which has the responsibility for inculturation, always with the review of the Apostolic See, so that the unity of the Church is not wounded in its highest and most perfect manifestation, the celebration of the Sacred Liturgy.

---

[10] *Sacramentum Caritatis*, n. 54.
[11] *Ibid.*
[12] *Ibid.*

Personal Conditions for Eucharistic Participation

What is required for my own "fruitful participation"[13] in the Sacred Liturgy? First of all, there must be conversion of life to Christ. "Active participation in the Eucharistic Liturgy can hardly be expected if one approaches it superficially, without an examination of his or her life."[14] The Holy Father mentions three specific means by which the conversion of life necessary for participation in the Holy Mass is cultivated: "Recollection and silence for at least a few moments before the beginning of the liturgy,"[15] the Eucharistic fast, and sacramental Confession. Active participation in the Eucharistic Sacrifice necessarily means active participation "in the life of the Church as a whole, including a missionary commitment to bring Christ's love into the life of society."[16]

We participate most fully in the Holy Mass when we personally receive our Lord in Holy Communion. Presence at the Holy Mass, however, does not confer "a right or even an obligation to approach the table of the Eucharist."[17] If a person cannot receive Holy Communion, for whatever reason, he is still required to participate in the Holy Mass. His participation "remains necessary, important, meaningful and fruitful."[18] Pope Benedict XVI urges the faithful, who find themselves in a situation in which they cannot receive Holy Communion, "to cultivate a desire for full union with

---

[13] *Sacramentum Caritatis*, n. 55.
[14] *Ibid.*
[15] *Ibid.*
[16] *Ibid.*
[17] *Ibid.*
[18] *Ibid.*

Christ through the practice of spiritual communion, praised by Pope John Paul II and recommended by saints who were masters of the spiritual life."[19]

Participation by Non-Catholic Christians

May "Christians belonging to churches and ecclesial communities not in full communion with the Catholic Church"[20] participate in Holy Communion? First of all, Pope Benedict XVI observes that the "intrinsic link between the Eucharist and the Church's unity inspires us to long for the day when we will be able to celebrate the Holy Eucharist together with all believers in Christ."[21] But we must remember that the Holy Eucharist signifies full communion with the Church. The Holy Eucharist cannot, therefore, become our means of trying to achieve a unity which does not exist. "We hold that eucharistic communion and ecclesial communion are so linked as to make it generally impossible for non-Catholic Christians to receive the former without enjoying the latter."[22]

In the same way, concelebration with ministers who are not in full communion with the Church contradicts the meaning of the Eucharistic Sacrifice. Once again, such concelebration signifies full communion with the Church, which is not verified in the case of the ministers in question.

In individual cases, however, for the sake of the salvation of souls, non-Catholic Christians may receive Holy Communion, the absolution of their sins in the Sacrament of

---

[19] *Ibid.*
[20] *Sacramentum Caritatis*, n. 56.
[21] *Ibid.*
[22] *Ibid.*

congregation and a large number of concelebrating priests. He underlines the importance of such celebrations "when the bishop himself celebrates, surrounded by his presbyterate and by the deacons."[33] It is clear that such celebrations require very careful planning, so that the distinct manner of participation by priests and by the other members of the faithful is reflected.

Within the discussion of large-scale celebrations of the Sacred Liturgy, Pope Benedict XVI addresses the question of the use of the Latin language at large-scale international gatherings. The Holy Father, making his own a proposal made by the Synod of Bishops, declares that, "with the exception of the readings, the homily and the prayer of the faithful, such liturgies could be celebrated in Latin."[34] The practice of celebrating the Mass in Latin would "express more clearly the unity and the universality of the Church."[35] In addition, he mandates that "the better-known prayers of the Church's tradition should be recited in Latin and, if possible, selections of Gregorian chant should be sung."[36]

In order to further the appropriate use of Latin in the Sacred Liturgy, the Holy Father asks that seminarians be educated "to understand and to celebrate the Mass in Latin, and also to use Latin texts and execute Gregorian chant."[37] It should also be observed that, if the faithful are to be able to participate more fully in large international liturgical celebrations, in which the Latin language and Gregorian Chant are appropriately employed, they will need to be introduced

---

Sacramentum Caritatis, n. 61.
Sacramentum Caritatis, n. 62.
Ibid.
Ibid.
Ibid.

Penance, and the Anointing of the Sick, but specific conditions must be present. Those conditions are clearly stated in the Code of Canon Law and the *Catechism of the Catholic Church*.

Participation through the Communications Media

With regard to the televised celebration of the Holy Mass, Pope Benedict XVI underlines the grave responsibility to make the celebration an example of the correct and reverent offering of the Holy Mass. The Holy Father mentions also the importance of paying careful attention to the fittingness of the place in which the televised Mass is celebrated.[23]

Participation in the Holy Mass by way of television does not fulfill the Sunday and Holy Day obligation to participate in the Eucharistic Sacrifice. The televised Mass represents the celebration of the Mass but does not make it present. Certainly, for those who are unable physically to attend Holy Mass, the viewing of the Mass on television or listening by radio is most commendable. But it is clear, too, that for those who are able to attend Mass, watching the Sunday Mass does not "dispense (us) from going to church and sharing in the Eucharistic assembly in the living Church."[24]

Participation by the Sick

Our Holy Father addresses with special attention a concern that he notes was often expressed during the sessions of the Synod of Bishops: the pastoral care of the sick, whether they

---

[23] Cf. *Sacramentum Caritatis*, n. 57.
[24] *Ibid.*

are at home or in the hospital. He states directly: "These brothers and sisters of ours should have the opportunity to receive sacramental communion frequently."[25] He reminds us that sacramental Communion will unite them more fully to Christ in their suffering and help them to carry out their mission in the Church "by the offering of their sufferings in union with our Lord's sacrifice."[26]

Regarding persons with special needs, the parish should provide for their participation in the Holy Mass, if their situation makes it possible. The church building should be provided with those structures which make it accessible to persons with special needs.[27]

Regarding the mentally impaired, Eucharistic Communion should be given to them, "if they are baptized and confirmed." The Holy Father reminds us that the mentally handicapped "receive the Eucharist in the faith also of the family or the community that accompanies them."[28]

Prisoners and the Reception of Holy Communion

Pope Benedict XVI recalls the Gospel injunction to visit prisoners, found in our Lord's Parable of the Last Judgment, and its fitting inclusion in the corporal works of mercy. He observes that those in prison "have a particular need to be visited personally by the Lord in the Sacrament of the Eucharist."[29]

In the isolation of imprisonment, the closeness of our Lord

---

[25] *Sacramentum Caritatis*, n. 58.
[26] *Ibid.*
[27] Cf. *Ibid.*
[28] *Ibid.*
[29] *Sacramentum Caritatis*, n. 59.

and of the Church through the reception of Holy Communion assists the prisoner greatly in keeping a Christian mind and heart, and in working toward "full social rehabilitation." The Holy Father declares: "Taking up the recommendation of the Synod, I ask dioceses to do whatever is possible to ensure that sufficient pastoral resources are invested in the spiritual care of prisoners."[30]

Migrants and Eucharistic Participation

A particular pastoral care must be exercised on behalf of migrants. Pope Benedict XVI expresses a special concern for migrants who belong to the Eastern Catholic Churches, for "in addition to being far from home, they also encounter the difficulty of not being able to participate in the eucharist liturgy in their own rite."[31] He asks that they be served priests of their proper rites.

In this regard, the Holy Father reminds us of the spiritual enrichment which comes to us through ou munication with persons of the other rites in the Ch notes the particular enrichment which comes to p deacons from knowing different liturgical rites. note, the Holy Father recommends that semina troduced to these traditions."[32]

Large-Scale Concelebration and the

The Holy Father addresses briefly the large celebration of the Holy Mass wi

---

[30] *Ibid.*
[31] *Sacramentum Caritatis*, n. 60.
[32] *Sacramentum Caritatis*, note 180.

to both the prayers in Latin and the Gregorian Chant in their parish churches.

Small-Group Celebrations

Pope Benedict XVI acknowledges the benefit of a small-group celebration of the Holy Mass, especially for formation in an active and fruitful participation in the Eucharistic Sacrifice. He cautions, however, that such celebrations be coherent "with the overall pastoral activity of the diocese."[38] Clearly, they cannot be seen, in any way, to be "in competition with, or parallel to, the life of the particular Church."[39] The Holy Father sets forth "necessary criteria" for small-group celebrations. First, they must serve the unity of the local community and not contribute to its fragmentation. Second, the benefits reaped "ought to be clearly evident."[40] And, lastly, the fruitful participation of the whole assembly should be fostered, and "the unity of the liturgical life of individual families" should be safeguarded.[41] In other words, as much as possible, families should be able to take part together in the Eucharistic Sacrifice.

---

[38] *Sacramentum Caritatis*, n. 63.
[39] *Ibid.*
[40] *Ibid.*
[41] *Ibid.*

- 18 -

Eucharistic Participation and Interior Dispositions

Pope Benedict XVI concludes Part Two of *Sacramentum Caritatis* by taking up two topics: 1) the deeply interior dispositions required for a fruitful participation in the Holy Eucharist; and 2) eucharistic adoration and devotions. Both topics address what is required for a personal eucharistic piety, which is deep and constant. Both topics have suffered from some neglect during the first decades of the liturgical reforms that followed upon the Second Vatican Ecumenical Council.

Clearly, the whole meaning of participation in the Eucharistic Sacrifice is union with Christ in the outpouring of His life for love of God and of our brothers and sisters. "The Church's great liturgical tradition teaches us that fruitful participation in the liturgy requires that one be personally conformed to the mystery being celebrated, offering one's life to God in unity with the sacrifice of Christ for the salvation of the whole world."[1] Otherwise, participation in the Holy Mass becomes a mere matter of words and gestures which are not related to the everyday living of the faithful.

To cultivate union with Christ in the Holy Eucharist, one must be carefully instructed in eucharistic faith and

---

[1] *Sacramentum Caritatis*, n. 64.

that instruction must be kept fresh. How is such instruction imparted and consistently deepened? Following upon the recommendations formulated at the Synod of Bishops, Pope Benedict XVI indicates "a mystagogical approach to catechesis"[2] as the most fitting method of formation in eucharistic faith. Mystagogy refers to the instruction given to the newly baptized, that they may deepen their understanding of the faith in which they have been baptized. Without mystagogy, there is a great danger that the newly baptized will cease to grow in the faith and its practice, and may even drift from the faith so recently received. The mystagogical approach helps the faithful to continue, throughout a lifetime, deepening their understanding of the reality and action of the Holy Mass.

Our Holy Father reminds us again of "the close relationship between the *ars celebrandi* (the art of celebrating) and an *actuosa participatio* (active participation)."[3] It follows then that the manner of the celebration of the Eucharistic Sacrifice is key to the deepening of interior participation. Pope Benedict XVI observes: "By its nature, the liturgy can be pedagogically effective in helping the faithful to enter more deeply into the mystery being celebrated."[4] In accord with the long tradition of the Church, the preparation for Baptism or reception into the full communion of the Church involves a gradual introduction into the rites of the Sacred Liturgy. The instruction in the doctrine of the faith is necessarily accompanied by the experience of the doctrine alive in the Sacred Liturgy and in the witness of those who have come to life in Christ through the sacraments.

---

[2] *Ibid.*
[3] *Ibid.*
[4] *Ibid.*

Three Elements of the Mystagogical Approach

In the ongoing instruction in Eucharistic faith, there are three elements which must be respected. The first is the interpretation of the rites of the Sacred Liturgy in terms of the story of our salvation. Christ is the fullness of all revelation. In Him, everything revealed in the Old Testament finds its fulfillment. In the Holy Eucharist, His consummation of God's plan for our salvation on Calvary is always present for us. The great reality of Christ's Real Presence with us in the Holy Eucharist is more deeply understood in the light of all of the Holy Scriptures. "From the beginning, the Christian community has interpreted the events of Jesus' life, and the Paschal Mystery in particular, in relation to the entire history of the Old Testament."[5]

Secondly, the mystagogical approach is always attentive to teaching the meaning of the various signs employed in the Sacred Liturgy. Pope Benedict XVI points out the particular importance of teaching the meaning of liturgical signs in a highly technological culture which is weakened in its ability to interpret these signs. "More than simply conveying information, a mystagogical catechesis should be capable of making the faithful more sensitive to the language of signs and gestures which, together with the word, make up the rite."[6]

Thirdly, a mystagogical catechesis always draws out the meaning of the liturgical rites for our daily Christian living in all of its aspects. Pope Benedict XVI draws particular attention to the missionary meaning of our participation

---

[5] *Ibid.*
[6] *Ibid.*

in the Holy Eucharist. "Part of the mystagogical process is to demonstrate how the mysteries celebrated in the rite are linked to the missionary responsibility of all the faithful."[7] Through the mystagogical approach, the participant in the Holy Eucharist becomes ever more aware of how the Rite of the Mass must transform us more and more into effective witnesses of Christ in the world.

Finally, our Holy Father reminds us that such high quality of catechesis requires teachers and mentors who are fittingly prepared. The bishops at the synod also "called for greater involvement by communities of consecrated life, movements and groups which, by their special charisms, can give new impetus to Christian formation."[8] Pope Benedict XVI reminds us that the Holy Spirit is most generous in bestowing His sevenfold gift for "the apostolic mission of the Church, which is charged with spreading the faith and bringing it to maturity."[9]

Reverence for the Holy Eucharist

If Eucharistic faith is cultivated and deepened, the sign will be a greater reverence before the whole action of the Mass. Such reverence will be manifest in the outward signs which those who are accompanying the new Christians or new members of the Church teach them. The Holy Father comments: "I am thinking in general of the importance of gestures and posture, such as kneeling during the central moments of the Eucharistic Prayer."[10] Every gesture and

---

[7] *Ibid.*
[8] *Ibid.*
[9] *Ibid.*
[10] *Sacramentum Caritatis*, n. 65.

posture, every outward sign, should point to the reality that God Himself comes to us on earth "in the lowliness of the sacramental signs."[11]

---

[11] *Ibid.*

- 19 -

Celebration and Adoration

Pope Benedict XVI describes, as one of the most moving moments of the Synod of Bishops, the gathering of the bishops, together with a large number of the faithful, for Eucharistic adoration in Saint Peter's Basilica. The fact that Eucharistic adoration is essentially related to participation in the Eucharistic Sacrifice explains its great attraction for us.[1]

Our Holy Father comments on a certain loss of understanding and appreciation of Eucharistic adoration in the years following the Second Vatican Ecumenical Council. He recalls an argument used to discourage Eucharistic adoration, namely, the argument that the Sacred Host was given to us "not to be looked at, but to be eaten."[2] He also notes how the Church's long tradition points up the fallacy of such an argument. Saint Augustine, for instance, teaches us that we would sin by not adoring the Most Blessed Sacrament, the Body and Blood of Christ.

Eucharistic adoration "is simply the natural consequence of the Eucharistic celebration, which is itself the Church's supreme act of adoration."[3] Eucharistic adoration is truly

---

[1] Cf. *Sacramentum Caritatis*, n. 66.
[2] *Ibid.*
[3] *Ibid.*

an extension of the highest adoration which we give during the celebration of the Eucharistic Sacrifice. "The act of adoration outside Mass prolongs and intensifies all that takes place during the liturgical celebration."[4] The failure to participate in Eucharistic adoration is a sign of the loss of Eucharistic faith. It should not surprise us that the fruit of the abandonment of Eucharistic adoration in many parts of the Church, in the years immediately following the Second Vatican Ecumenical Council, has resulted in a loss of Eucharistic faith. Today, we are told that a significant number of those who call themselves Catholic do not believe that the bread and wine are changed into the Body and Blood of Christ during the Eucharistic Sacrifice and remain the Body of Christ reposed in the tabernacle.

Eucharistic Adoration

Pope Benedict XVI, therefore, urges "the practice of eucharistic adoration, both individually and in community."[5] He reminds us that, if Eucharistic adoration is to be fruitfully practiced, then its profound significance, especially in relationship to the Eucharistic Sacrifice, must be taught. "Great benefit would ensue from a suitable catechesis explaining the importance of this act of worship, which enables the faithful to experience the liturgical celebration more fully and more fruitfully."[6]

The Holy Father then gives two concrete recommendations for fostering the development of Eucharistic adora-

---

[4] *Ibid.*
[5] *Sacramentum Caritatis*, n. 67.
[6] *Ibid.*

tion. First, he specifically recommends the establishment of perpetual or continuous adoration of the Most Blessed Sacrament in "specific churches or oratories," especially in "densely populated areas."[7] Secondly, he recommends that children who are preparing to receive First Holy Communion "be taught the meaning and the beauty of spending time with Jesus, and helped to cultivate a sense of awe before his presence in the Eucharist."[8] With many Eucharistic chapels established throughout dioceses, every child preparing for First Holy Communion can be effectively introduced to the practice of Eucharistic adoration. Certainly, children and young people should be invited to join the whole community in keeping the hours of Eucharistic adoration.

In the context of promoting continuous or perpetual Eucharistic adoration, Pope Benedict XVI expresses his deepest gratitude to "all those institutes of consecrated life whose members dedicate a significant amount of time to eucharistic adoration" and to "associations of the faithful and confraternities specifically devoted to eucharistic adoration."[9] The Holy Father observes that "they serve as a leaven of contemplation for the whole Church and a summons to individuals and communities to place Christ at the center of their lives."[10] The Church is greatly blessed in religious communities which practice continuous adoration of the Most Blessed Sacrament.

---

[7] *Ibid.*
[8] *Ibid.*
[9] *Ibid.*
[10] *Ibid.*

Forms of Eucharistic Adoration

Our relationship with our Lord Jesus Christ always leads us back to His Real Presence in the Most Blessed Sacrament and, in Him, to all our brothers and sisters for whom He gave His life. Rightly then, the Church urges the corporate adoration of the Most Blessed Sacrament. "For this reason, besides encouraging individual believers to make time for personal prayer before the Sacrament of the Altar, I feel obliged to urge parishes and other church groups to set aside times for collective adoration."[11]

The Holy Father also mentions other forms of Eucharistic adoration. Processions with the Blessed Sacrament are an important way to promote and deepen Eucharistic faith. Pope Benedict XVI notes that "already existing forms of eucharistic piety retain their full value."[12] He mentions, in particular, the annual procession on the Solemnity of Corpus Christi, parish Forty Hours devotions, "local, national and international Eucharistic Congresses, and other similar initiatives."[13]

Placement of the Tabernacle

Pope Benedict XVI concludes Part Two of *Sacramentum Caritatis* by discussing "the proper placement of the tabernacle in our churches."[14] He observes that the "correct positioning of the tabernacle contributes to the recognition of

---

[11] *Sacramentum Caritatis*, n. 68.
[12] *Ibid.*
[13] *Ibid.*
[14] *Sacramentum Caritatis*, n. 69.

Christ's real presence in the Blessed Sacrament."[15] He notes that "the place where the eucharistic species are reserved, marked by a sanctuary lamp, should be readily visible to everyone entering the church."[16]

The architecture of the church, therefore, will help us to determine the proper location of the tabernacle, so that it will be central and immediately visible to all who enter the church. With regard to already existing churches, Pope Benedict XVI notes that, "where the high altar with its tabernacle is still in place, it is appropriate to continue to use this structure for the reservation and adoration of the Eucharist, taking care not to place the celebrant's chair in front of it."[17] With regard to new churches, the Blessed Sacrament Chapel, if there is one, should be "close to the sanctuary."[18] If there is no Blessed Sacrament Chapel, "it is preferable to locate the tabernacle in the sanctuary, in a sufficiently elevated place, at the center of the apse area, or in another place where it will be equally conspicuous."[19]

Finally, Pope Benedict XVI reminds us of the care which is to be given to the artistic beauty of the tabernacle. He also reminds us that "final judgment on these matters belongs to the diocesan bishop."[20]

---

[15] *Ibid.*
[16] *Ibid.*
[17] *Ibid.*
[18] *Ibid.*
[19] *Ibid.*
[20] *Ibid.*

Becoming Whom We Receive
in Holy Communion

In Part Three of the Post-synodal Apostolic Exhortation *Sacramentum Caritatis*, Pope Benedict XVI discusses all that the Holy Eucharist means for our daily living. He begins the treatment by quoting a passage from the "Bread of Life Discourse" of our Lord Jesus Christ, recorded in Chapter 6 of the Gospel according to Saint John. The passage reads: "As the living Father sent me, and I live because of the Father, so he who eats me will live because of me" (*Jn* 6:57). The import of our Lord's words is clear. His true Body which we receive in the Holy Eucharist, by its very nature, becomes the principle and pattern of our daily living. We not only believe in the Holy Eucharist and celebrate the Holy Eucharist, but we also live by and through the Holy Eucharist.

Our Holy Father recalls a passage from the *Confessions* of Saint Augustine regarding the Holy Eucharist. Saint Augustine writes about the different effect of consuming the Heavenly Bread of the Holy Eucharist in comparison with the effect of eating earthly food. Earthly food is assimilated into our very being; it becomes a part of us. The Body of Christ, the Heavenly Food of our earthly pilgrimage, on the contrary, transforms us into the Food we consume, that is, Christ Whom we receive in Holy Communion.

Spiritual Worship

The Holy Eucharist "expresses at once both the origin and the fulfilment of the new and definitive worship of God."[1] Participation in the Holy Eucharist is the most perfect action of worship which we can offer to God. It is, in fact, God the Father's most perfect gift to us in our Lord Jesus Christ. At the same time, it is the fullness of our Christian life, for, in the Eucharistic Sacrifice, we unite our hearts, our lives, fully with Christ, pouring out our life in selfless and ever purer love, that is, Christlike love.

Pope Benedict XVI quotes Saint Paul's exhortation that our "spiritual worship" be, indeed, the presentation of our "bodies as a living sacrifice, holy and acceptable to God" (*Rom* 12:1). Our worship of God is never distant from or detached from our bodily existence. In the Eucharistic Sacrifice, rather, we, together with the whole Church, offer our bodies through, with and in our Lord Jesus Christ. Referring to paragraph 1368 of the *Catechism of the Catholic Church*, our Holy Father reminds us: "Catholic doctrine, in fact, affirms that the Eucharist, as the sacrifice of Christ, is also the sacrifice of the Church, and thus of all the faithful."[2] In the Eucharistic Sacrifice, our whole being is lifted up to the glorious Christ Who pours out His life for us, in order that we be transformed by pouring out our lives.

---

[1] *Sacramentum Caritatis*, n. 70.
[2] *Ibid*.

Transformation of Every Aspect of Life

Our spiritual worship, that is, our participation in the Holy Eucharist, "includes and transfigures every aspect of life."[3] In everything we think and say and do, we are to give glory to God and serve our neighbor. The Holy Eucharist gives us the strength to live a totally Christlike life. "There is nothing authentically human—our thoughts and affections, our words and deeds—that does not find in the Sacrament of the Eucharist the form it needs to be lived to the full."[4]

Through our participation in the Eucharistic Sacrifice, we come to understand that we cannot compartmentalize any aspect of our life, in order to keep it from the transforming grace of Christ's Real Presence. The Holy Eucharist, therefore, is always first and most important in our daily living and in our whole life. It must never be seen as detached from or unrelated to any part of our life. "Worship pleasing to God thus becomes a new way of living our whole life, each particular moment of which is lifted up, since it is lived as part of a relationship with Christ and as an offering to God."[5] Making visits to the Blessed Sacrament during the day and making a spiritual Communion at various moments throughout the day are true and efficacious devotional expressions of the reality of the Holy Eucharist which transforms every aspect of our lives.

---

[3] *Sacramentum Caritatis*, n. 71.

[4] *Ibid.*

[5] *Ibid.*

Living the Lord's Day

The Sunday Mass obligation is the discipline which respects the truth that the origin and the highest expression of our life in Christ is the Holy Eucharist. The obligation is a very ancient discipline of the Church. Our Holy Father quotes Saint Ignatius of Antioch who describes Christians as "those living in accordance with the Lord's Day."[6] In Pope Benedict XVI's words: "The Christians' customary practice of gathering on the first day after the Sabbath to celebrate the resurrection of Christ—according to the account of Saint Justin Martyr—is also what defines the form of a life renewed by an encounter with Christ."[7]

The observance of Sunday as the Lord's Day and as the first day of the week expresses our consciousness of what the Holy Eucharist means in our life. It changes our life completely and gives a new meaning to all time. Each gift of time from our Lord is understood as an invitation to offer ourselves with Christ in love. Keeping the Lord's Day, in the words of Pope Benedict XVI, "means living in the awareness of the liberation brought by Christ and making our lives a constant self-offering to God, so that his victory may be fully revealed to all humanity through a profoundly renewed existence."[8]

Our Holy Father points out that a carelessness or lack of interest in keeping the Lord's Day is dangerous for our Christian living. "To lose a sense of Sunday as the Lord's Day,

---

[6] Saint Ignatius of Antioch, *Ad Magnesios*, 9, 1: *Patrologia Graeca* 5, 670, in: *Sacramentum Caritatis*, n. 72.

[7] *Sacramentum Caritatis*, n. 72.

[8] *Ibid.*

a day to be sanctified, is symptomatic of the loss of an authentic sense of Christian freedom, the freedom of the children of God."[9] Because of who we are in Christ, our conscience demands that we keep the Sunday Mass obligation. At the same time, participation in the Sunday Eucharist forms and strengthens our conscience to know what is good and to avoid what is evil.

Pope Benedict XVI then recalls for us the Apostolic Letter *Dies Domini* of Blessed Pope John Paul II. Blessed Pope John Paul II, in fact, called Sunday by four names: the Day of the Lord, the Day of Christ, the Day of the Church, and the Day of Man. It is the Day of the Lord because it marks the completion of God's creation. The offering of the Holy Eucharist embraces and permeates all of creation, as Blessed Pope John Paul II reminded us.[10] It is the Day of Christ because, in the Holy Eucharist, God gives us the grace of becoming the new creation, of living in Christ. It is the Day of the Church, for the whole body of disciples marks the day by coming together to participate in the Holy Eucharist. Finally, it is the Day of Man, for it brings us "joy, rest and fraternal charity."[11]

Finally, regarding the Lord's Day, Pope Benedict XVI comments on the fittingness of concentrating parish activities around Sunday Mass. The Holy Father reminds us that, notwithstanding the granting of the indult to celebrate Sunday Mass on the Saturday evening, it is Sunday that is to be made holy.

---

[9] *Sacramentum Caritatis*, n. 73.
[10] Cf. *Ecclesia de Eucharistia*, n. 8.
[11] *Sacramentum Caritatis*, n. 73.

Sunday and Resting from Work

Sunday, the Lord's Day, is to be a day of rest from work. The Holy Father expresses the hope that civil society will recognize the need of the Christian to take Sunday rest and not punish him for it. By taking a rest from work, the Christian, in fact, sees work in its proper perspective, that is, as a means to give glory to God and to serve one's neighbor. Sunday Mass helps us to recognize always that "work is for man and not man for work."[12]

Sunday rest helps us to avoid what Pope Benedict XVI terms enslavement to work. "It is on the day consecrated to God that men and women come to understand the meaning of their lives and also of their work."[13]

Sunday Celebrations in the Absence of a Priest

When there is no priest to offer Sunday Mass, what should an individual Christian and the whole Christian community do? First of all, we should make a thorough search to know the times of Masses at neighboring churches and should proceed to participate in Mass at a neighboring church.

If the distance to a neighboring church with a priest is so great that it is not possible for the faithful to travel there, the local community is encouraged to gather and to give praise and worship to God, as they are able. Care must be taken, however, that the community understands that its gathering

---

[12] *Sacramentum Caritatis*, n. 74.
[13] *Ibid.*

for prayer does not fulfill the Sunday obligation, for it is not the celebration of the Holy Mass.[14]

The Conference of Bishops is to make available the rite to be followed, lest the faithful confuse the celebration of prayer in the absence of a priest with the full Sunday Eucharist. The lay faithful who conduct a Sunday liturgy in the absence of priests are to follow carefully the rite set down by the Conference of Bishops. Our Holy Father cautions that care be taken, lest the gathering of the community on the Lord's Day without the presence of the priest "create confusion about the central role of the priest and the sacraments in the life of the Church."[15]

Given the key part which the Sunday Mass has in our Christian identity, we must be careful to maintain a clear and strong sense of our life in the Church and of the irreplaceable service of the priest who acts in the person of Christ, the Head and Shepherd of the flock. Our Holy Father reminds us that occasions when the faithful gather on Sunday in the absence of a priest "should be privileged moments of prayer for God to send holy priests after his own heart."[16]

Pope Benedict XVI recalls Blessed Pope John Paul II's 1979 *Letter to Priests*, in which he recalled a certain practice of the faithful who are deprived of a priest by a "dictatorial regime." The faithful would meet at the church or at a shrine. They would place on the altar a priest's stole which they had saved. Then, they would recite the prayers of the Mass. When they came to the words of consecration,

---

[14] Cf. *Sacramentum Caritatis*, n. 75.

[15] *Ibid.*

[16] *Ibid.*

they halted in silence because these words can only be uttered with efficaciousness by a priest. By keeping silence at the time when the consecration would normally take place the faithful expressed their heartfelt desire for a priest who would offer the Holy Mass for them, once again.[17]

Sunday Mass and
Membership in the Church

Participation in Sunday Mass keeps before our eyes the reality that Christ's Eucharistic Sacrifice makes us one community, makes us to live for Christ and, therefore, to live for one another. Pope Benedict XVI comments on what he calls the vertical and horizontal sense of our participation in the Communion of the Saints through the Holy Eucharist. Vertically, we, with all the saints, have communion with God in the Holy Mass. Horizontally, we, with all the saints, are made one with each other through the Eucharistic Sacrifice. Each time that we are privileged to participate in the Eucharistic Sacrifice, we are joined by the angels and all the saints. This is why, when we participate in Holy Mass, we invoke the intercession of the Blessed Virgin Mary and all the saints.

Through Baptism, we are brought to life in Christ. Baptism cleanses us from all sin, and we become members of the Church, the Mystical Body of Christ. The Holy Eucharist nourishes the life of Christ within us, from the moment of our baptism, and therefore draws us more intensely into the life of the Church.

---

[17] Cf. *Ibid.*

The Holy Father comments on how the individual Christian experiences what the Holy Eucharist means by participation in the life of the diocese and the parish. Referring to a passage from Saint Paul's *Letter to the Romans* (14:8), Pope Benedict XVI also notes how associations of the faithful, ecclesial movements and institutes of the consecrated all "have a particular responsibility for helping to make the faithful conscious that they *belong* to the Lord."[18]

The radical secularization of our culture has led many to be isolated from others. It has eroded our sense of belonging to one another in the Church. The diocese and the parish, and all associations of the faithful, conscious of the effects of secularization, must work to overcome isolation and the loss of a sense of belonging. "Christianity, from its very beginning, has meant fellowship, a network of relationships constantly strengthened by hearing God's word and sharing in the Eucharist, and enlivened by the Holy Spirit."[19]

---

[18] *Sacramentum Caritatis*, n. 76.
[19] *Ibid.*

- 21 -

The Holy Eucharist and Everyday Life

When considering the Holy Eucharist as a mystery to be lived, it is important, in our day, to recognize how our totally secularized culture has alienated everyday life from the Christian faith. The Holy Eucharist, however, by its very nature, animates every aspect of our lives. Through the Sacrament of the Holy Eucharist, Christ is in our midst to bring us to life in the Holy Spirit. "Hence the Holy Eucharist, as the source and summit of the Church's life and mission, must be translated into spirituality, into a life lived 'according to the Spirit' (*Rom* 8:4ff.; cf. *Gal* 5:16, 25)."[1] One who receives the Body of Christ with faith thinks with Christ and acts as Christ would act. Quoting verse 2 of the twelfth chapter of Saint Paul's Letter to the Romans, Pope Benedict XVI declares: "In this way the Apostle of the Gentiles emphasizes the link between true spiritual worship and the need for a new way of understanding and living one's life."[2]

Because Communion with Christ in the Holy Eucharist involves every aspect of daily living, it necessarily involves the commitment to address the Word of Christ to the other

---

[1] *Sacramentum Caritatis*, n. 77.
[2] *Ibid.*

cultures we encounter. The Holy Eucharist leads us to evangelize all cultures, for Christ pours out His life for the salvation of all men and women. "The Eucharist becomes a criterion for our evaluation of everything that Christianity encounters in different cultures."[3] The Holy Eucharist, for instance, must be our inspiration and strength in evangelizing the Islamic culture which becomes ever more present in our society and the world. Everything in life must be seen in the light of the Holy Eucharist, in order to see each thing in truth and to act in all things with love.

The Holy Eucharist and the
Spirituality of the Lay Faithful

Pope Benedict XVI then applies the truth about the relationship of the Holy Eucharist to everyday living to the various states of life. He begins by considering the spirituality of the lay faithful. He reminds us that the Holy Eucharist "meets each of us as we are, and makes our concrete existence the place where we experience daily the radical newness of the Christian life."[4] The Holy Eucharist nourishes in us the life of Christ, which we have received through Baptism, inspiring and strengthening us to live our baptismal vocation, that is, to do whatever God asks of us, especially in what pertains to our vocation in life.

The vocation of the lay faithful, received at Baptism, is the sanctification and, therefore, the transformation of every human activity, the transformation of the world. Through the Sacrament of Confirmation, the grace of Baptism is strengthened and increased for the carrying out of the lay vocation.

---

[3] *Sacramentum Caritatis*, n. 78.
[4] *Sacramentum Caritatis*, n. 79.

The Holy Eucharist is the food which sustains the lay apostle in carrying out his or her mission. Pope Benedict XVI urges that the lay faithful "should cultivate a desire that the Eucharist have an ever deeper effect on their daily lives, making them convincing witnesses in the workplace and in society at large."[5] Recognizing the challenge of their vocation and the irreplaceable source of strength to meet the challenge in the Holy Eucharist, the lay faithful rightly treasure the possibility of participating in Holy Mass daily, if possible.

Knowledge and love of the Eucharistic mystery is especially critical to the vocation of the married and for the family life begun with the exchange of marriage consent. Through participation in the Holy Mass and in Eucharistic devotion, husband and wife come to understand the essential marks of their love of each other. The love of Christ poured out in the Holy Eucharist is the source of their love which, by definition, is total, ever faithful, and open to the procreation of new human life. The relationship between parents and children, likewise, finds its model in the purest and most selfless love of Christ in the Eucharistic Sacrifice.

Our Holy Father concludes the discussion of the Holy Eucharist and the spirituality of the laity by urging parish priests to "unfailingly support, guide and encourage the lay faithful to live fully their vocation to holiness within this world which God so loved that He gave His Son to become its salvation (cf. *Jn* 3:16)."[6] The principal means by which pastors of souls assist those called to marriage and the family in this regard are instruction in the truth regarding the Holy Eucharist and exhortation to love of the Holy Eucharist.

---

[5] *Ibid.*

[6] *Ibid.*

The Holy Eucharist and Priestly Spirituality

In writing about the relationship of the Holy Eucharist to the spiritual life of the priest, Pope Benedict XVI recalls striking words from the Rite of Ordination of a Priest. After the new priest has been consecrated by the Laying on of Hands and the Prayer of Ordination, he goes before the Bishop for the Anointing of Hands and the Handing over of the Bread and Wine. When the Bishop hands over the bread and wine, he declares: "Receive the oblation of the holy people, to be offered to God. Understand what you do, imitate what you celebrate, and conform your life to the mystery of the Lord's Cross."[7] In other words, the priest is to live the mystery of Christ's Sacrifice in his daily life.

The priest is to make the Holy Eucharist the center of His priestly life and the source of His priestly ministry. The spiritual life is, therefore, "his highest priority."[8] He is to bring Christ to the people, and, therefore, He must know Christ intimately and have the closest possible communion with Christ. He must experience deeply the love of Christ in the Holy Eucharist, if he is to love the flock in the person of Christ the Head and Shepherd, Who lays down His life for the sheep (*Jn* 10:11).

Given the inherent Eucharistic nature of the priest's spirituality, Pope Benedict XVI makes his own a recommendation made by the Bishops at the Synod of 2005, namely, that the priest should celebrate Mass every day, even if no faithful are present for the celebration. The Holy Father comments:

---

[7] *The Roman Pontifical, Rites of Ordination of a Bishop, of Priests and of Deacons*, Ordination of a Priest, n. 163, in *Sacramentum Caritatis*, n. 80.

[8] *Sacramentum Caritatis*, n. 80.

"This recommendation is consistent with the objectively infinite value of every celebration of the Eucharist, and is motivated by the Mass's unique spiritual fruitfulness."[9] Through the daily celebration of the Holy Eucharist, at which the whole Communion of Saints always assists, the priest identifies ever more clearly His ministry and is strengthened to carry it out.

The Holy Eucharist and the
Spiritual Life of Consecrated Persons

Those called to the consecrated life are to follow Christ more closely, especially in the evangelical counsels of poverty, chastity and obedience. Their life consecrated totally to Christ is a source of light and strength for all the faithful in their Christian living. Acknowledging the variety of services which are provided by consecrated persons in the Church, Pope Benedict XVI reminds us that the distinct gift of consecrated persons is not so much what they do but who they are in Christ for the whole Church. "The essential contribution which the Church expects from consecrated persons is much more in the order of being than of doing."[10]

The Holy Father addresses at some length "the importance of the witness of virginity, precisely in its relation to the mystery of the Eucharist."[11] Consecrated virginity is a sign of the "Church's exclusive devotion to Christ, whom she accepts as her Bridegroom with a radical and fruitful fidelity."[12] For the consecrated virgin, who belongs totally

---

[9] *Ibid.*
[10] *Sacramentum Caritatis*, n. 81.
[11] *Ibid.*
[12] *Ibid.*

to Christ and is fittingly called the bride of Christ, participation in the Holy Mass and Eucharistic devotion is the most elevated and most treasured exercise of her vocation. With regard to her being in the Church, the consecrated virgin finds in the Holy Eucharist "encouragement and strength to be a sign, in our own times too, of God's gracious and fruitful love for humanity."[13]

The consecrated life is for all of us a sign of our final destiny, that is, participation in the Wedding Feast of the Lamb, sharing in the indescribable riches of eternal life with Christ. In a particular way, the consecrated virgin, from the earliest times of the Church, has by a solemn rite been constituted "a sacred person, a surpassing sign of the Church's love for Christ, and an eschatological image of the world to come and the glory of the heavenly bride of Christ."[14] Thus consecrated life, and consecrated virginity in particular, remind us that everything in our lives should be viewed in the light of Heaven, the point of arrival of our earthly pilgrimage. Each time we participate in the Holy Eucharist, that point of arrival is anticipated, and we are reminded, indeed given a pledge, of our ultimate heritage, that is, eternal life with God—Father, Son and Holy Spirit—in the company of the angels and all the saints.

---

[13] *Ibid.*

[14] *The Roman Pontifical*, "Consecration to a Life of Virginity," Introduction, n. 1.

- 22 -

The Holy Eucharist and
Moral Transformation

We all know the challenge of Christ-like living in a totally secularized society. It requires supernatural strength to overcome the many temptations to let ourselves be enslaved, to let ourselves "live as if God did not exist," as Blessed Pope John Paul II used to say. The Holy Eucharist is the font of energy to live in freedom, to love as Christ loves, purely and selflessly. Pope Benedict XVI refers us to his Encyclical Letter *Deus Caritas Est*, in which he reminded us that participation in the Eucharistic Sacrifice necessarily issues in a daily life marked by "the concrete practice of love."[1]

Our Holy Father goes on to comment that the moral transformation inherent in Eucharistic Communion is not a mere matter of a moral injunction imposed upon us by participation in the Eucharistic Sacrifice. "It is before all else the joy-filled discovery of love at work in the hearts of those who accept the Lord's gift, abandon themselves to Him and thus find true freedom."[2] It is our intimacy with the Lord in the Holy Eucharist which, at one and the same time, makes us conscious of our own sinfulness and inflames our desire to live always in Christ and, therefore, to love as He loves.

---

[1] *Deus Caritas Est*, n. 14, in *Sacramentum Caritatis*, n. 82.
[2] *Ibid.*

To help us understand the moral transformation which heartfelt participation in the Holy Eucharist brings about, Pope Benedict XVI refers us to the story of Zacchaeus (*Lk* 19:1–10). When Zacchaeus met our Lord, he was at once moved to confess his sinfulness, to make superabundant restitution for what he had stolen, and to provide from his substance for the poor. Our Holy Father concludes: "The moral urgency born of welcoming Jesus into our lives is the fruit of gratitude for having experienced the Lord's unmerited closeness."[3]

Eucharistic Consistency

Pope Benedict XVI concludes his presentation on the moral transformation worked by the Holy Eucharist by reflecting on the public nature of our Eucharistic worship, that is, its "consequences for our relationships with others."[4] Receiving Holy Communion is never a merely private act. Because of our public communion with Christ in the Holy Eucharist, others rightly expect Christlike living from us. If we receive Holy Communion and then think, speak, and act in a way which betrays Christ, then we give scandal to others. We lead them to think that it is all right to receive Christ into our souls and, at the same time, to ignore or contradict His teaching by the way we live. We deceive them regarding the holiness of the Most Blessed Sacrament and its involvement in every aspect of our being and life.

Participation in the Holy Eucharist demands that all of us give witness to the truth and love which Christ teaches us. The responsibility to give public witness to our faith is especially weighty for those "who, by virtue of their social or political position, must make decisions regarding fundamen-

---

[3] *Ibid.*
[4] *Sacramentum Caritatis*, n. 83.

tal goods, such as respect for human life, its defense from conception to natural death, the family built upon marriage between a man and a woman, the freedom to educate one's children and the promotion of the common good in all its forms."[5] The Holy Father addresses in particular Catholic politicians, who, in virtue of their communion with Christ in the Holy Eucharist, must promote and support laws which respect the natural law written by God on every human heart.[6] We are witnesses to the scandal caused by Catholic politicians who present themselves to receive Holy Communion and, at the same time, consistently support legislation which violates the natural moral law—for example, legislation which permits procured abortion, human cloning, embryonic stem-cell research, euthanasia or "assisted suicide," so-called "same-sex marriage," and other violations of fundamental human rights. Regarding such situations, the Holy Father, referring to chapter 11 of Saint Paul's *First Letter to the Corinthians*, declares plainly: "There is an objective connection here with the Eucharist (cf. *1 Cor* 11:27–29)."[7]

The Holy Father reminds Bishops of their duty to reaffirm the relationship of the Holy Eucharist to the moral life, especially for those who have responsibility for the common good. For Bishops to do less constitutes a failure to shepherd the flock entrusted into their care.

The Holy Eucharist and the Church's Mission

Pope Benedict XVI reminds us that the love of God, given to us in the Holy Eucharist, is not a gift for us alone but rather, by its very nature, is to be shared with others, indeed

---

[5] *Ibid.*
[6] Cf. *Ibid.*
[7] *Ibid.*

with all. Even as we recognize how much we need God's love in our lives and how wonderfully He gives us the gift of His love in the Holy Eucharist, so also we recognize that our whole world needs most the gift of God's love and that we are the messengers and instruments of Divine Love. "What the world needs is God's love; it needs to encounter Christ and to believe in him."[8]

The Holy Eucharist is an incomprehensible gift of God's love which fills us with gratitude and with the desire to make this most wonderful gift, our Lord Jesus Himself, known to all our brothers and sisters. If, as is true, the Holy Eucharist is the source and summit of the Church's life, the Holy Eucharist is also the source and summit of the Church's mission in the world.

The missionary nature of the Holy Eucharist is manifest in the celebration of the Last Supper. Our Lord Jesus, on the night before He died, instituted the Holy Eucharist so that His Sacrifice on Calvary, which would be consummated on the following day, might be celebrated in every time and place, and for all men. Reflecting upon the Lord's Supper, Pope Benedict XVI declares:

> At the Last Supper, Jesus entrusts to his disciples the sacrament which makes present his self-sacrifice for the salvation of us all, in obedience to the Father's will. We cannot approach the eucharistic table without being drawn into the mission which, beginning in the very heart of God, is meant to reach all people. Missionary outreach is thus an essential part of the eucharistic form of the Christian life.[9]

---

[8] *Sacramentum Caritatis*, n. 84.
[9] *Ibid.*

The First and Fundamental
Mission: To Bear Witness

The first and fundamental mission which we accept by our participation in the Holy Eucharist is to bear witness to the mystery of God's love by the manner of our living. What does it mean to bear witness? Pope Benedict XVI provides the answer: "We become witnesses when, through our actions, words and way of being, Another makes himself present."[10] God depends upon our witness to bring His love to all men, but the gift is His, not ours. We are His messengers and instruments. While God trusts us to be His witnesses, we pray for the grace to honor God's trust by becoming more and more like His Divine Son Who is "the faithful and true witness (cf. *Rev* 1:5; 3:14), the one who came to testify to the truth (cf. *Jn* 18:37)."[11] We pray that we may be true witnesses, that is, that Christ may make Himself present to others through all our thoughts and words and deeds.

Pope Benedict XVI reflects upon the great desire of the early Christians to bear the ultimate witness, namely, to offer their lives in martyrdom. In martyrdom, the early Christians rightly saw the most complete obedience to the command of Saint Paul that we should offer our bodies in pure spiritual worship (cf. *Rom* 12:1). By martyrdom, in the words of Saint Ignatius of Antioch, we become "Christ's pure bread." In other words, the martyr unites himself perfectly with Christ in the Eucharistic Sacrifice and thus becomes, in Christ, spiritual food for the whole Church. Even as we are called to become the Eucharist we receive, to become more and more

---

[10] *Sacramentum Caritatis*, n. 85.
[11] *Ibid*.

like Christ, so the martyr, in a preeminent way, becomes the Eucharist which he or she has received.

Our Holy Father reminds us that, also in our time, the Church is blessed with martyrs who offer their lives in faithful witness to God. He also reminds us that, although we do not anticipate being put to death because of our witness to God, "we know that worship pleasing to God demands that we should be inwardly prepared for it."[12] If we are attentive to the call to be faithful in witness, even to the shedding of our blood, then we will offer each day "the joyful and convincing testimony of a consistent Christian life, wherever the Lord calls us to be his witnesses."[13]

Witness to Christ, Our Only Savior

The more we come to know and love our Eucharistic Lord, the more we understand our mission of bringing our Lord to the world. As Pope Benedict XVI reminds us, we do not offer to the world "just a theory or a way of life inspired by Christ, but the gift of his very person."[14]

Today, there is a strong tendency to make our witness acceptable to a world which is marked by a great diversity of peoples and beliefs. The Holy Eucharist reminds us that our testimony must be a clear witness to the person of our Lord Jesus Christ and the salvation which He alone brings to the world. In other words, our witness must be a sound and uncompromising proclamation of the truth about our Lord Jesus Christ. It must be given with the conviction that

---

[12] *Ibid.*
[13] *Ibid.*
[14] *Sacramentum Caritatis*, n. 86.

it is what the world most needs and what will serve most the common good.

In this connection, the Holy Father addresses the situation of those who carry out the Church's mission "in areas where Christians are a minority or where they are denied religious freedom."[15] Pope Benedict XVI calls to mind places in the world in which fidelity to Sunday Mass is heroic, for it subjects the faithful to the danger of exclusion and violence. He points out that "wherever religious freedom is lacking, people lack the most meaningful freedom of all, since it is through faith that men and women expresses their deepest decision about the ultimate meaning of their lives."[16] He invites us to pray for religious freedom throughout the world.

The Holy Eucharist Offered to the World

Our Lord Jesus Christ makes it clear that He has come to save all men, without boundary or exclusion. During His public ministry, he showed "his deep compassion for every man and woman."[17] He revealed fully and perfectly the desire of God the Father that all may have life in Him. In the Eucharistic Sacrifice, our Lord makes always new the outpouring of His life for all, including those who had falsely condemned Him and put Him to death.

One with Christ in the Eucharistic Sacrifice, we accept our mission to love all our brothers and sisters, without boundary or exclusion. Participation in the Holy Eucharist means loving others as God loves them. Pope Benedict XVI quotes a text from his Encyclical Letter *Deus Caritas Est* to describe

---

[15] *Sacramentum Caritatis*, n. 87.
[16] *Ibid.*
[17] *Sacramentum Caritatis*, n. 88.

the nature of Eucharistic charity. He tells us that it "consists in the very fact that, in God and with God, I love even the person whom I do not like or even know."[18] How can we practice such charity? Because we have met our Lord Jesus in Holy Communion, we have received Him into our very being, and therefore we look upon our brothers and sisters with His eyes, with the eyes of the One Who gave His life for us, loving us all "to the end" (*Jn* 13:1).

The body of disciples, gathered at the altar of Christ's Sacrifice, is also deeply conscious of its responsibility to bring Christ to every local community and to our world. Union with Christ in the Eucharistic Sacrifice commits us "to work for the building of a more just and fraternal world."[19]

Pope Benedict XVI earlier reminded us, "The love that we celebrate in the sacrament is not something we can keep to ourselves. By its very nature it demands to be shared with all."[20] Our encounter with the Real Presence of Christ in the Holy Eucharist stirs up in us the desire to make Him known to others, especially to those who have not heard of Him or who, for whatever reason, have forgotten and abandoned Him Whom once they knew and loved.

The Holy Eucharist and Reconciliation

The Holy Eucharist, because it is communion with Christ, has a profound meaning for our social relations. Communion with our Eucharistic Lord commits us to work for reconciliation in all our relationships. Pope Benedict XVI makes reference to the Sermon on the Mount and the spe-

---

[18] *Deus Caritas Est*, n. 18, in *Sacramentum Caritatis*, n. 88.
[19] *Sacramentum Caritatis*, n. 88.
[20] *Sacramentum Caritatis*, n. 84.

cific command of our Lord regarding the necessity of reconciliation for fitting worship: "So if you are offering your gift at the altar, and there remember that your brother has something against you, leave your gift there before the altar and go; first be reconciled to your brother, and then come and offer your gift" (*Mt* 5:23–24).

Through our communion with Him in the Holy Eucharist, our Lord urges us to be reconciled, to be committed both to good communication with others and to just relations. Holy Communion is the Heavenly Food which transforms injustices and serves good order in all our relations and in society in general.

Pope Benedict XVI raises the question of the involvement of the Church in politics. He acknowledges that "it is not the proper task of the Church to engage in the political work of bringing about the most just society possible," but he also observes that "nonetheless she cannot and must not remain on the sidelines in the struggle for justice."[21]

The Church has two specific tasks in promoting the struggle for justice. First, she must be a voice of reason to argue for a just resolution of every question. Secondly, she must be the instrument by which man becomes spiritually strong to make the sacrifices necessary to preserve and foster justice. Pope Benedict XVI calls all the faithful to be agents in the promotion of the respect for the inviolable dignity of human life: "Precisely because of the mystery we celebrate, we must denounce situations contrary to human dignity, since Christ shed his blood for all, and at the same time affirm the inestimable importance of each individual person."[22]

---

[21] *Sacramentum Caritatis*, n. 89.
[22] *Ibid.*

Globalization and Stewardship

Our Holy Father notes specific questions of justice, which our participation in the Holy Eucharist inspires and strengthens us to address, for example a globalization which increases "the gap between the rich and the poor worldwide."[23] There is also the failure to practice good stewardship of the earth's resources, so that they serve the needs of all. He writes also of the "huge camps . . . of displaced persons and refugees, who are living in makeshift conditions in order to escape a worse fate, yet are still in dire need."[24] He reflects on the very large sums of money expended worldwide for armaments, while so many are living in poverty.

Our participation in the Holy Eucharist makes us conscious of our "clear and disquieting responsibility"[25] for the situations of injustice in which our brothers and sisters suffer: "The food of truth demands that we denounce inhumane situations in which people starve to death because of injustice and exploitation, and it gives us renewed strength and courage to work tirelessly in the service of the civilization of love."[26]

Calling to mind the concern of the first Christians to place their goods at the service of all, especially those in most need, Pope Benedict XVI underlines the importance of our weekly collections at Sunday Mass. He also highlights the works of the Church's charitable institutions, like Catholic Charities, which concretely address the needs of the poorest among us. Regarding these institutions, he declares: "Inspired by the

---

[23] *Sacramentum Caritatis*, n. 90.
[24] *Ibid.*
[25] *Ibid.*
[26] *Ibid.*

Eucharist, the sacrament of charity, they become a concrete expression of that charity; they are to be praised and encouraged for their commitment to solidarity in our world."[27]

The Church's Social Teaching

All of us, and in particular the lay faithful, bear a most heavy responsibility for the economic, political and social conditions in our society. The questions of justice which we confront are complex and do not admit of easy responses. It is therefore essential that we receive instruction in the Church's social doctrine. Pope Benedict XVI reminds us that the Church's history, from her beginnings, is rich with lessons in social justice. He cautions against "misguided compromises or false utopias," and underlines the "realism and moderation"[28] of the Church's social teaching.

Treating the relationship of the Holy Eucharist to the Church's social teaching, Pope Benedict XVI notes, in particular, the implications of the Eucharistic Sacrifice for our approach to creation. The very offering of bread and wine remind us of God's plan for the world. Pope Benedict XVI corrects false notions of the world in strong terms: "The world is not something indifferent, raw material to be utilized simply as we see fit. Rather, it is part of God's good plan, in which all of us are called to be sons and daughters in the one Son of God, Jesus Christ (cf. *Eph* 1:4–12)."[29]

Through the Holy Eucharist, we participate already in the new creation which Christ will bring to full realization at His Second Coming. The new creation is not yet; we are

---

[27] *Ibid.*

[28] *Sacramentum Caritatis*, n. 91.

[29] *Sacramentum Caritatis*, n. 92.

called to prepare for it each day of our lives. We prepare for it by our knowledge of God's plan for our world and by our respect and obedience before God's plan.

We await the Final Coming of our Lord. Pope Benedict XVI concludes: "Our Christian life, nourished by the Eucharist, gives us a glimpse of that new world—new heavens and a new earth—where the New Jerusalem comes down from heaven, from God, 'prepared as a bride adorned for her husband' (*Rev* 21:2)."[30]

Eucharistic Compendium

Our Holy Father concludes Part Three of *Sacramentum Caritatis* by announcing his acceptance of a proposal made by the Bishops in Synod, namely the preparation of a *Compendium* on the Holy Eucharist. According to the mind of the Bishops, the *Compendium* is to be "a means of helping the Christian people to believe, celebrate and live ever more fully the mystery of the Eucharist."[31]

The *Compendium Eucharisticum* was published by the Congregation for Divine Worship and the Discipline of the Sacraments in 2009.[32] It contains "texts from the *Catechism of the Catholic Church*, prayers, explanations of the Eucharistic Prayers of the Roman Missal and other useful aids for a correct understanding, celebration and adoration of the Sacrament of the Altar."[33] Pope Benedict XVI expressed the hope that the *Compendium* would have two effects in the Church

---

[30] *Ibid.*

[31] *Sacramentum Caritatis*, n. 93.

[32] Congregation for Divine Worship and the Discipline of the Sacraments, *Compendium Eucharisticum* (Vatican City State: Libreria Editrice Vaticana, 2009).

[33] *Sacramentum Caritatis*, n. 93.

and in our individual Christian lives. First, he hoped that it "will help make the memorial of the Passover of the Lord increasingly the source and summit of the Church's life and mission." Secondly, he hoped that it "will encourage each member of the faithful to make his or her life a true act of spiritual worship."[34]

Running the Race Before the Cloud of Witnesses

Pope Benedict XVI concludes his Post-synodal Apostolic Exhortation *Sacramentum Caritatis* by reminding us that "the Eucharist is at the root of every form of holiness, and each of us is called to the fullness of life in the Holy Eucharist."[35] To illustrate the Eucharistic foundation of our life in Christ, he recalls the names of many saints who attained heroic sanctity of life by way of strong Eucharistic devotion. The heart of their heroic sanctity was the Sacrament of the Holy Eucharist.

Our Holy Father, accordingly, declares that the Eucharistic mystery "needs to be firmly believed, devoutly celebrated and intensely lived in the Church."[36] In the Holy Eucharist, we discover that the fulfillment of our life is found in the participation in the life of God—Father, Son and Holy Spirit —which our Lord Jesus, God the Son made man, offers to us. Our religious life is deeply personal. It is a relationship with God the Father in God the Son through the outpouring of the Holy Spirit into our very being. It is through participation in the Eucharistic Sacrifice and through Eucharistic

---

[34] *Ibid.*
[35] *Sacramentum Caritatis*, n. 94.
[36] *Ibid.*

devotion that we draw ever closer to our Lord Jesus and receive from Him the gift of divine Trinitarian life.

In the Holy Eucharist, we offer our own lives with Christ, we draw near to Christ with "the whole community of believers," and we express "our solidarity with all men and women,"[37] for whom Christ offers up His life in the Eucharistic Sacrifice. Pope Benedict XVI "asks all pastors to spare no effort in promoting an authentically eucharistic Christian spirituality."[38] He expresses confidence that priests, deacons and extraordinary ministers of Holy Communion will carry out their service with due preparation and attentive care, and therefore find in their Eucharistic ministry the inspiration and strength which they need to grow in holiness of life.

Addressing all of the lay faithful and especially families, Pope Benedict XVI urges them to find in the Eucharistic Sacrifice "the energy needed to make their lives an authentic sign of the presence of the risen Lord."[39] Addressing consecrated men and women, he urges them to make the Eucharist the center of their lives, and thereby to manifest to all the great beauty of a life dedicated totally to Christ.

Intercession of the Martyrs and All the Saints

Pope Benedict XVI recalls the story of the martyrs of Abitinae in North Africa, at the beginning of the fourth century. The Roman Emperor had forbidden the celebration of the Holy Mass. Certain Christians in North Africa defied the Emperor's prohibition because they "felt bound to celebrate

---

[37] *Ibid.*

[38] *Ibid.*

[39] *Ibid.*

the Catholic faith with the enthusiasm and energy of the first disciples. He devoted the final years of his pontificate, his last energies, to presenting anew the truth about the Holy Eucharist. He urged Catholics to draw the enthusiasm and energy for the new evangelization from the Holy Eucharist, from the Real Presence of Christ in the Most Blessed Sacrament. He reminded the faithful that only by knowing Christ in the depth of the Eucharistic encounter would they be able to bring Christ to the world to transform it, in accord with God's all-merciful love.

In *Ecclesia de Eucharistia*, he described the wonder which should fill the mind and the heart of all who are privileged to participate in the offering of the Sacrifice of the Mass, a wonder which, above all, should fill the priest who acts in the person of Christ when he offers the Mass. At the Holy Mass, Christ's action, through the priest's ministry, truly unites Heaven and Earth, for it makes present the glorious Body, Blood, Soul and Divinity of Christ for the salvation of the world. In the Eucharistic Sacrifice, all of the faithful witness the mystery of the immense love of Our Lord Jesus Christ for all men, without boundary. It is the mystery which Our Lord expressed with His words, as He was dying upon the Cross for the salvation of the world: "I thirst." (*Jn* 19:28) Every time the faithful participate in the Holy Mass or worship the Blessed Sacrament outside of Mass they not only witness the thirst of Christ for souls, which is truly immeasurable and ceaseless, but they share in that thirst. Together with Christ, they express that thirst in the work of the new evangelization.

Sharing in the thirst of Christ for souls through the Holy Eucharist, the work of the new evangelization, which would otherwise be impossible, becomes possible for man. The re-ality of divine love makes it possible. Pope Benedict XVI tells us:

the Lord's Day."[40] They stated plainly that they could not live without the Holy Eucharist. As a result, they were martyred at Abitinae.

Our Holy Father asks the intercession of the martyrs of Abitinae and of all the saints. He asks that they teach us to be faithful to our Sunday encounter with the Risen Lord in the Holy Eucharist. He prays that we may imitate the martyrs of Abitinae, so that what we celebrate on the Lord's Day becomes the pattern of our daily living.

The Blessed Virgin Mary

In a special way, our Holy Father asks that the Blessed Virgin Mary be one with us as we go to meet our Lord each Sunday in the Holy Eucharist. Our Blessed Mother is, in the words of the Blessed Pope John Paul II, the "Woman of the Eucharist." The Virgin Mary leads us to the Holy Eucharist. She is with us in the Eucharistic Sacrifice, training our eyes to behold, with her, the great mystery of God the Father's love of us in Jesus Christ. At the Holy Mass, we pray through the intercession of the Blessed Virgin Mary, and strive to imitate her in the offering of her whole life in obedience to God the Father and for the good of the Church.

Our Blessed Mother is totally beautiful (*tota pulchra*); in her, we see the glory of God as it shines forth in a totally virtuous life. Pope Benedict XVI declares: "From Mary we must learn to become men and women of the Eucharist and of the Church, and thus to present ourselves, in the words of Saint Paul, 'holy and blameless' before the Lord, even

---

[40] *Sacramentum Caritatis*, n. 95.

as he wished us to be from the beginning (cf. *Col* 1:22; *Eph* 1:4)."[41]

The Conclusion of *Sacramentum Caritatis*

The Holy Father brings *Sacramentum Caritatis* to a close by asking the intercession of the Mother of God, so that the Holy Spirit will stir up in us anew the fire which the disciples on the road to Emmaus on Easter Sunday experienced when they encountered the Risen Lord in the Holy Eucharist. He notes how the "the splendor and beauty radiating from the liturgical rite"[42] should be for us a sign of the incomprehensible beauty of Christ's offering of His life for us sacramentally, of God's immense and ceaseless love of us in our Lord Jesus Christ.

The Holy Eucharist makes us realize that our Lord is with us always, and therefore brings us true and lasting joy. "True joy is found in recognizing that the Lord is still with us, our faithful companion along the way. The Eucharist makes us discover that Christ, risen from the dead, is our contemporary in the mystery of the Church, his body."[43]

Finally, Pope Benedict XVI expresses the desire that we encourage one another to encounter our Lord in the Holy Eucharist, and therefore to proclaim the truth which we have discovered in the Eucharist, the truth declared by our Lord before His Ascension to the right hand of the Father: "Lo, I am with you always, until the end of the world" (*Mt* 28:20).

---

[41] *Sacramentum Caritatis*, n. 96.
[42] *Sacramentum Caritatis*, n. 97.
[43] *Ibid.*

Conclusion

Bringing to conclusion these reflections upon Blessed Pope John Paul II's last Encyclical Letter, *Ecclesia de Eucharistia* and Pope Benedict XVI's Post-synodal Apostolic Exhortation *Sacramentum Caritatis*, I call to mind once again the fundamental and wonderful truth about the Holy Eucharist as it was expressed by the Fathers at the Second Vatican Ecumenical Council. Making reference to the teaching of Saint Thomas Aquinas, they simply declared: "For in the Most Holy Eucharist is contained the entire spiritual good of the Church."[1] Blessed Pope John Paul II, in *Ecclesia de Eucharistia*, expressed the same truth about the Most Blessed Sacrament. He reminded us that the life of the Church has i[...] "foundation and well-spring" in the Sacred Triduum—[...] days of Christ's Passion, Death, and Resurrection—w[...] is fully contained in the Eucharistic Mystery. As he [...] the Paschal Triduum "is as it were gathered up, fo[...] owed and 'concentrated' for ever in the gift of [...] Eucharist."[2]

Throughout his lengthy pontificate, Blessed [...] Paul II tirelessly addressed the enduring an[...] truths of the Catholic faith to the seculariza[...] ing relativism of contemporary culture. He [...] faithful to transform culture through the [...] evangelization, that is by professing, ce[...]

---

[1] Vatican Council II, Decree *Presbyterorum*
[2] *Ecclesia de Eucharistia*, n. 5.

[I]n the sacrament of the Eucharist, Jesus shows us in particular the *truth about the love* which is the very essence of God. It is this evangelical truth which challenges each of us and our whole being. For this reason, the Church, which finds in the Eucharist the very center of her life, is constantly concerned to proclaim to all, *opportune importune* (cf. 2 *Tim* 4:2), that God is love. Precisely because Christ has become for us the food of truth, the Church turns to every man and woman, inviting them freely to accept God's gift.[3]

How much our attitudes, words and actions should give witness to the truth of the Holy Eucharist, the Mystery of Faith, which, at its every celebration, embraces the entire world with divine love!

In his last letter to priests on the occasion of Holy Thursday in 2004, referring to his last Encyclical Letter *Ecclesia de Eucharistia* and to his book written on the occasion of his 50th anniversary of priesthood ordination, Blessed Pope John Paul II contemplated the mystery of the ordained priesthood in its essential relationship to the Eucharistic mystery. Blessed Pope John Paul II declared to his brother priests:

Before this extraordinary reality we find ourselves amazed and overwhelmed, so deep is the humility by which God "stoops" in order to unite himself with man! If we feel moved before the Christmas crib, when we contemplate the Incarnation of the Word, what must we feel before the altar where, by the poor hands of the priest, Christ makes his Sacrifice present in time? We can only fall to our knees and silently adore this supreme mystery of faith.[4]

---

[3] *Sacramentum Caritatis*, n. 2.
[4] "Letter of the Holy Father Pope John Paul II to Priests for Holy Thursday 2004," n. 2.

The humble adoration of the ordained priest before the mystery of the Most Blessed Sacrament inspires a similar response from all of the faithful before the reality of the Sacrifice of the Mass. Pope Benedict XVI, in his letter inaugurating the Year for Priests, described how this was so in the life of the Curé of Ars, Saint John Mary Vianney:

> Saint John Mary Vianney taught his parishioners primarily by the witness of his life. It was from his example that they learned to pray, halting frequently before the tabernacle for a visit to Jesus in the Blessed Sacrament. . . . This way of educating the faithful *to the Eucharistic presence and to communion* proved most effective when they saw him celebrate the Holy Sacrifice of the Mass. Those present said that "it was not possible to find a finer example of worship. . . . He gazed upon the Host with immense love."[5]

It is my fervent prayer that the reflections on *Ecclesia de Eucharistia* and *Sacramentum Caritatis* contained in these pages will lead the reader to an ever deeper and more ardent knowledge and love of our Eucharistic Lord. May humble adoration of the Eucharistic Mystery be the inspiration and strength for a Eucharistic life, a life of pure and selfless love of our neighbor, especially our brothers and sisters who are in most need.

May the Blessed Virgin Mary, woman of the Eucharist, lead us to her Son in the Holy Sacrifice of the Mass. Encountering the Real Presence of Christ in the Most Blessed Sacrament, through the divine maternity of the Blessed Virgin Mary, may we always heed her maternal counsel to us: "Do whatever he tells you." (*Jn* 2:5)

---

[5] Pope Benedict XVI, "Letter Proclaiming a Year for Priests on the 150th Anniversary of the 'Dies Natalis' of the Curé of Ars," June 16, 2009.

Bibliography

Benedict XVI, Pope. Christmas Message to the Roman Curia, "Christmas, the Council and conversion in Christ,"
L'Osservatore Romano, Weekly Edition in English, January
4, 2006, pp. 4–6.

———. Encyclical Letter *Deus Caritas Est*, "On Christian
Love," December 25, 2005.

———. "Letter Proclaiming a Year for Priests on the 150th
Anniversary of the 'Dies Natalis' of the Curé of Ars,"
June 16, 2009.

———. Post-synodal Apostolic Exhortation *Sacramentum
Caritatis*, "On the Eucharist as the Source and Summit
of the Church's Life and Mission," February 22, 2007.

Congregation for Divine Worship and the Discipline of the
Sacraments. *Compendium Eucharisticum*, Vatican City
State: Libreria Editrice Vaticana, 2009.

———. Instruction *Redemptionis Sacramentum*, "On Certain
Matters to Be Observed or to Be Avoided Regarding the
Most Holy Eucharist," March 25, 2004.

John Paul II, Pope Blessed. Apostolic Letter *Mane Nobiscum Domine*, "For the Year of the Eucharist," October
7, 2004.

———. Encyclical Letter *Ecclesia de Eucharistia*, "On the
Eucharist in its Relationship to the Church," April 17,
2003.

———. "Letter to Priests for Holy Thursday 2004," March 28, 2004.

———. Post-synodal Apostolic Exhortation *Christifideles Laici*, "On the Vocation and the Mission of the Lay Faithful in the Church and in the World," December 30, 1988.

Vatican Council II. Austin Flannery, O.P., editor. *Vatican Council II: The Conciliar and Post Conciliar Documents*, Collegeville, Minn.: Liturgical Press, 1975.

Glossary

ACTIVE PARTICIPATION: the part taken by the faithful in the celebration of the Holy Mass. Such participation, while it includes various external expressions, is above all interior, consisting in the offering of one's own self in union with the sacrifice of Christ, and being united with Him in the reception of Holy Communion.

ANAMNESIS: a Greek term for "calling to mind," referring to the remembrance of Christ's death and resurrection which is a part of every Eucharistic prayer

CHURCH: the society founded by Jesus Christ, made up on earth of those who have been baptized and who follow the teachings of the Apostles and their successors the bishops, under the authority of the Bishop of Rome. While the Church is a visible, hierarchically ordered society in this world (Church militant), she also includes the saints in Heaven (Church triumphant) and the souls in Purgatory (Church suffering).

COMMUNION: the sharing in spiritual goods which unites the members of the Church with God and with each other. In a particular way, the term refers to the reception of the Holy Eucharist, which brings us the most perfect union with God and with one another.

EUCHARIST: the greatest of the Sacraments instituted by Jesus Christ. In the Eucharist, through His priests, Jesus Christ changes bread and wine into His Body and Blood in order to make present among us the sacrifice of Calvary, to feed us with Himself, and to remain with us always. The Eucharist is therefore the source and summit of the Church's life.

EUCHARISTIC ADORATION: prayer before Jesus Christ Who remains present in the Sacred Host under the appearance of bread. Adoration can take place before the Eucharist exposed publicly in a monstrance, or it can be done in private visits to the Blessed Sacrament reserved in the tabernacle.

INCULTURATION: the assimilation of a particular culture into the life of the Church, especially in the liturgy. Inculturation involves both the use of those cultural elements which are compatible with the Gospel, and the purification or transformation of those which are not.

MYSTAGOGY: further instruction in the faith given to those already baptized. Mystagogy focuses in a particular way on conveying a deeper understanding of the sacraments, especially the Holy Eucharist.

NEW EVANGELIZATION: the proclamation of the Gospel in parts of the world which have historically been Christian, but which have become secularized. It requires professing, celebrating, and living the Catholic faith with the enthusiasm and energy of the first disciples.

PRIESTLY CELIBACY: the state of remaining unmarried, in perfect and perpetual continence, as a sign of interior dedication to Christ and the Church, which is freely embraced by candidates for the priesthood. This commitment, which is made by all candidates for the priesthood in the Latin Rite, is based on the example of Christ Himself, the Spouse of the Church.

REAL PRESENCE: the Presence of Jesus Christ, with His Body, Blood, Soul, and Divinity, in the sacrament of the Holy Eucharist, in a way which is real and substantial, not merely symbolic.

RESERVED BLESSED SACRAMENT: the Consecrated Hosts which are kept in the tabernacle after the conclusion of the Mass. Because Christ remains present as long as the Consecrated Host exists, the faithful can and should adore Him in the Reserved Blessed Sacrament. The Reserved Blessed Sacrament can also be used for the distribution of Holy Communion, whether during or outside of Mass.

SACRIFICE: the offering of some good to God, in order to adore Him, give Him thanks, make atonement for sins, or ask for His favor. The only sacrifice truly worthy of God is Christ's offering of His life on the Cross, which is renewed in the sacrifice of the Eucharist.

SPIRITUAL COMMUNION: the expression of an interior desire to receive Christ in the Holy Eucharist, when one is unable to receive Holy Communion. The prayer of spiritual communion deepens our interior union with Christ, and prepares us for the next time we are able to receive Holy Communion.

TRANSUBSTANTIATION: the term used by the Church's tradition to express the truth that, at the Consecration of the Mass, the substance of the bread and wine are completely transformed into the Body and Blood of Jesus Christ, together with His Soul and His Divinity. Only the "accidents" (external appearances and properties) of bread and wine remain.

VIATICUM: Holy Communion given to those close to death. The word means "provision for the journey," because

Christ in the Blessed Sacrament accompanies the soul in its journey from this world to the next.

VICAR OF CHRIST: traditional Catholic title for the Roman Pontiff (the Pope). The title expresses the fact that as successor of St. Peter, to whom Jesus Christ gave authority over His Church on earth (*Mt* 16:18–19; *Jn* 21:15–17), the Pope represents Christ's authority on earth in a unique way.

About the Author

Raymond Leo Burke was born in Richland Center, Wisconsin, on June 30, 1948. He attended high school at Holy Cross Seminary in La Crosse, Wisconsin, before attending The Catholic University of America in Washington, D.C., where he studied as a Basselin Scholar (1968–1971). He undertook his studies in preparation for ordination to the Holy Priesthood at the Pontifical Gregorian University in Rome (1971–1975), and was ordained to the priesthood by Pope Paul VI on June 29, 1975, at the Basilica of Saint Peter in Rome.

Father Burke's first assignment was as Associate Rector of the Cathedral of Saint Joseph the Workman in La Crosse. In 1977, he received the additional duty of teaching religion at Aquinas High School in La Crosse. In 1980, Father Burke returned to Rome to study Canon Law at the Pontifical Gregorian University. In April 1984, after completing his studies, he was named Moderator of the Curia and Vice Chancellor of the Diocese of La Crosse.

In 1989, Father Burke returned to Rome, where Blessed Pope John Paul II named him Defender of the Bond of the Supreme Tribunal of the Apostolic Signatura. After five years at this post, the Holy Father appointed him Bishop of the Diocese of La Crosse on December 10, 1994. Bishop Burke was ordained to the episcopacy by Blessed Pope John Paul II on January 6, 1995, at the Basilica of Saint Peter, and was installed in the Diocese of La Crosse on February 22, 1995. During his years as Bishop of La Crosse, Bishop Burke founded the Shrine of Our Lady of Guadalupe.

On December 2, 2003, Bishop Burke was named Archbishop of Saint Louis. Archbishop Burke was installed in Saint Louis on January 26, 2004.

Archbishop Burke solemnly consecrated to the Most Sacred Heart of Jesus first the Diocese of La Crosse and then the Archdiocese of Saint Louis. In the Cathedral Basilica of Saint Louis, Archbishop Burke created a shrine dedicated to the Most Sacred Heart of Jesus.

On June 27, 2008, His Holiness Pope Benedict XVI appointed Archbishop Burke Prefect of the Supreme Tribunal of the Apostolic Signatura. On November 20, 2010, Pope Benedict XVI elevated him to the College of Cardinals of the Holy Roman Church. After his elevation to the College of Cardinals, His Holiness appointed Cardinal Burke as member of the Congregation for Bishops, the Congregation for Divine Worship and the Discipline of the Sacraments, and the Pontifical Council for Legislative Texts. In January 2011, His Holiness appointed Cardinal Burke as member of the Council of Cardinals and Bishops of the Section for Relations with States of the Secretariat of State.

Index